To The 'Hutchings'
from
'The Canadian Family Wrights'
Christmas 1969
—
Love Michael + Katrina

A CENTURY OF ART  Great Canadian Painting

EDITORIAL CONTRIBUTORS: *Paintings,* Elizabeth Kilbourn, Frank Newfeld; *Text,* Ken Lefolii / *Research,* William Kilbourn, Marjorie Harris, Sandra Scott

# Great

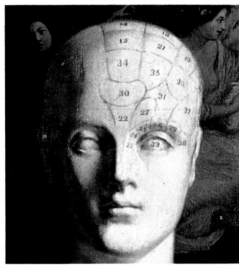

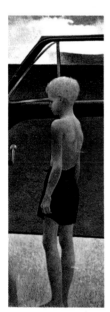

# Canadian Painting

A CENTURY OF ART / THE CANADIAN CENTENNIAL LIBRARY

# THE
# CANADIAN CENTENNIAL
# LIBRARY

Weekend
Magazine

McClelland
and Stewart
Limited

Pierre Berton, *Editor-in-Chief*
Frank Newfeld, *Art Director*
Ken Lefolii, *Managing Editor*

COVER
Emily Carr
*Reforestation*
1936 oil on canvas 44 x 27
McMichael Conservation
Collection of Art,
Kleinburg, Ontario

RIGHT
Michael Snow
*Walking Woman 61-62*
1961-2 oil on canvas 60 x 45
Avrom Isaacs, Toronto

# Contents

Cornelius Krieghoff
*The Blacksmith's Shop* / 1871   oil on canvas   22¹/₄ x 36¹/₄
Art Gallery of Toronto

# 1: The National Art

Painting is the national art of Canada in the same way and for some of the same reasons that hockey is the national game. For a youngster growing up in this raw dominion there has been, until very recently, far more to see and do than to say or hear. Artistic talent has turned naturally toward painting (as naturally as athletic talent has turned toward skating) and among people who have always been more interested in things than ideas the talent of landscape painters, particularly, has been seen and acknowledged. Most Canadians can name five native painters for every novelist, and ten or twenty painters for every poet, playwright or composer. Krieghoff, Walker and Watson, Morrice, Jackson, Carr, Riopelle and Town: these are the big names of Canadian culture, the stars of the serious arts. There are silk-screen copies of Canadian landscapes in thousands of rooms where the only book in sight is The Good One, and in this city-dwelling generation there are many Canadians for whom a moose is a heavy shape by Tom Thomson, the Laurentian Shield is a pile of paint by A. Y. Jackson, and a totem pole in the rain forest is a swirl of colour by Emily Carr.

There is a temptation to go further, to say that the painters who have shown us how to see the land have also shown us how to see ourselves. Looking back over the development of Canadian painting, the art historian and curator R. H. Hubbard has seen what he calls an "old tradition" of Canadianism: "directness, sober restraint and honest expression." There have certainly been Canadians who painted this way, but not many. In painting, as in most other things, Canada has always been a province of the Western world, never a capital. As fashions in art have changed in Europe and the U.S. they have changed—usually a little late—in Canada as well. Cornelius Krieghoff painted nineteenth-century Quebec farmers as though every habitant was a rosy, fun-loving German elf. Horatio Walker made the Ile d'Orléans look like the ancient soil of Provence; the Group of Seven gave the raw bush of northern Ontario the elegant outlines of art nouveau; Gerald Gladstone paints and sculpts space-age objects in a country that has never launched a space explorer of its own. And many—perhaps most—Canadian painters have been schooled in even less "sober, honest" fashions than these. John Fraser, the organizer of the Ontario Society of Artists in the 1870s, was a photo retoucher. Tom Thomson, the leading spirit just before World War I among the painters who later became the Group of Seven, was a letterer; Harold Town, the strongest talent of Painters Eleven in the 1950s, drew advertising illustrations. They were all commercial artists, whose job was to glamorize everything they touched; a slight tendency toward sober honesty will usually get a commercial artist fired.

Yet all these men have been exceptional painters. In their work, and in the work of many other good painters who began as commercial artists, there is a fine perception of the Canadian landscape and the Canadian people. The trouble begins when the perception is broken down into words. A painter's work is meant to be seen, not said. The best way to discover what the painters of the last hundred years have perceived about Canada is to search out their paintings and look at them. This book is meant to be the next best way to do the same thing. There are 106 paintings reproduced here in colour, many more than have been gathered in a single book before. Some are celebrated works from private galleries; others are the rarely seen property of private collectors. Two—Michael Snow's *Mixed Feelings* and Harold Town's *Great Divide*—were still on the easel when the preparations for this book began, and were sent to the editors by the artists in preference to any of their earlier work. Like most other paintings in the book, they were included not because they help make any particular case about Canadian painting or painters but because the editors think they belong in this portable gallery of the most interesting paintings from Canada's first hundred years. Many or even most of the painters who fit this definition are here. Some, of course, are not; from Antoine Plamondon in the last century to Tony Urquhart in our own day, there have been more good painters at work in Canada than any single volume, including this one, can comfortably describe and display.

John Fraser
*The Rogers Pass* / 1886   oil on canvas   22 x 30
National Gallery of Canada

## 2: A Century of Painting

The first trained painter to work in Canada seems to have been a Récollet friar named Frère Luc, who painted baroque decorations for Quebec churches in the winter of 1670-71. During the next two hundred years a rare professional stands out here and there, like François Beaucourt or Wilhelm von Moll Berczy, but almost all the painting done in Canada was amateur—most of it by British engineering officers who painted in their spare time. The most vivid link between this long amateur period and the professionalism that later made painting Canada's national art was the Dutchman Cornelius Krieghoff. Before he came to Quebec in 1840 Krieghoff had been a kind of strolling performer in Europe; he was trained in both art and music, and sold paintings or songs depending on the market. In Canada he painted serious pictures, rough sketches he called potboilers, or store and hotel signs, again depending on the market. He had a few short bursts of prosperity but died without friends or money in 1872, and it was eighty years before his paintings began to be prizes at the great art auctions of London and New York.

The first sign that painting was here to stay in Canada came almost simultaneously with the first sign that Canada was here to stay. In 1867 John Fraser formed a Society of Canadian Artists in Montreal. The Society didn't last but Fraser did; five years later he formed the Ontario Society of Artists in Toronto, now the oldest institution of its kind in the country. Fraser was a Scot who had studied art in London before he came to Canada. In Montreal he went to work for the inventive photographer William Notman, at first retouching photographs, then colouring them, and finally developing a revolutionary technique for tinting small camera portraits so cunningly that they were almost indistinguishable from miniature paintings. Fraser miniatures became a craze in Montreal society and Notman, who saw a chance to double a good thing, sent him to Toronto to open a branch of the business there. This was the beginning of Canadian painting's long embrace with commercial art. Fraser, who was painting landscapes on the side, slowly gathered a group of young painters around him, partly by giving them work in his commercial studio. In 1872 he formed them into the Ontario Society of Artists, and the next year gave the Society's first exhibition at the Notman and Fraser Gallery. Fraser hung two hundred and fifty paintings in a room fifty feet by thirty, and still jostled enough customers through the door to sell almost four thousand dollars' worth of paintings.

Sir John A. Macdonald and his great Liberal antagonist Edward Blake were both honorary members of the Society, and the then governor-general, the Earl of Dufferin, used to sketch with Society members in the Notman and Fraser Gallery on trips to Toronto. Art was in style as it has seldom been since. When the Marquis of Lorne with his wife, the Princess Louise, both amateur painters, arrived in 1880 to take over the governor-general's office, a delegation from Fraser's society persuaded him to sponsor a Royal Canadian Academy almost before he was off the boat. It took more than institutions to make painting the national art, but the institutions helped.

Unlike the academies of Europe, the RCA did not become the guardian of a particular style or theory of painting; for its first fifty years it was the home and meeting ground of almost all Canada's best serious artists. Fraser himself was a restless, aggressive man who made his photo gallery pay and sold illustrations to American magazines like *Scribner's*. But he was also one of the select group of painters invited to go west in 1886 on the CPR's first transcontinental trains. On this trip he painted *The Rogers Pass* (page 10) and a few other large pictures. A British critic said of them that Fraser was "possibly the inventor of a new school of landscape painting." Fraser's own opinion was warmer; he once stood in front of a Fraser landscape and said, "The man who can paint like that ought to wear a golden hat."

While Fraser was retouching photographs in Toronto, a young self-taught painter from Prince Edward Island named Robert Harris was in Boston trying to break into the newspaper business. His chance came when the *Evening Transcript* was caught without a woodcut of Henry Longfellow to illustrate a poem; Harris did the drawing overnight. Longfellow admired the likeness so much that he asked to meet young Harris, and told him that he should be painting portraits in oils. By the time he was thirty Harris had studied in Europe, returned to Canada and become the country's leading portrait painter, and joined the group who became founding members of the Royal Canadian Academy. But he was still a professional quick-sketch man, taking on assignments like one for the Toronto *Globe* to cover the trial of the men charged with the murder of the "Black" Donnellys. "The prisoners received me with

Robert Harris
*A Meeting of the School Trustees*
n.d.   oil on canvas   39¹/₄ x 48¹/₂
National Gallery of Canada

volleys of oaths and hid their faces under their coats," Harris wrote. But he "hung on until feeding time," and "got one old villain just as he was running through the wicket with a cake in one hand and a mug in the other . . . The jailer glanced at my book and burst out laughing at the likeness."

The same gift—for catching a likeness—won Harris the richest painter's prize of the 1880s, a four-thousand-dollar commission for a monumental painting of the Fathers of Confederation to hang in the parliament buildings. When the centre block went up in flames in 1916 the group portrait went with it, but Harris's sketches and later photographs of the finished canvas show that the painter's style and his subjects' were a close match: strong, plain, hard-headed. The painting Harris himself chose to exhibit at the Chicago World's Fair in 1893 was lost until a few years ago. *Harmony*, a small painting of a young woman playing the spinet (page 57), is a faithful reproduction of the feminine style and manner of late Victorian Montreal. Like his painting of the schoolmistress facing her trustees (page 13) it is a superb example of the North American realist tradition.

Harris was one of the few accomplished painters of that day who did no work, as far as anyone knows, for John Fraser's booming photograph "gallery." With the powerful dual attractions of the camera and the retoucher's brush—a new technology married to a new art—Notman and Fraser had the glamour of both ends of the television industry today. (Notman's partner in Montreal for a time was Henry Sandham, another leading painter, who later became an illustrator in Boston.) Up from the country and into the Notman and Fraser studios in the mid-70s came two Ontario farm boys, drawn by the romance of the big studio in the classic pattern of provincial aspiration. Horatio Walker was from Listowel; Homer Watson was from Doon; and in remarkably similar careers they became the pace-setting Canadian painters of the late nineteenth century.

They both left Canada during the 1880s to study, and they both eventually picked up techniques and ideas from the Barbizon school of landscape painters in France. (An American critic later said that Walker "out-Barbizoned" the Barbizon school.) In time they both settled in Canada, Watson in his native Doon and Walker on the Ile d'Orléans in Quebec. When Oscar Wilde visited Toronto in 1882 he called Watson "the Constable of Canada" after the great English landscape artist, and bought one of his paintings. Seduced by such high praise, Watson went to England for a long visit, and in his later paintings some critics see signs that he had set himself to out-Constable Constable. He painted *The Mill Ford* (page 34) in 1898. The setting is the valley of Doon in Ontario but it is hard to deny that the man, the animals, and the land itself might all be in Sussex or Kent. Watson knew Archibald Lampman, and once, after

Horatio Walker
*Oxen Drinking*
1899   oil on canvas   47$^1$/$_2$ x 35$^1$/$_2$
National Gallery of Canada

a conversation with the poet, wrote in his diary: "To me, Nature, the mother of life, speaks of a mighty region outside of man." In the 1920s, when painters like Watson and Walker had lost the limelight to the Group of Seven, the critic Hector Charlesworth leaped to their defence. "Academic persons who speak as if a distinctly Canadian school of landscape was only developed in the past five years," Charlesworth said, "are strangely ignorant of the work of such unmistakably native individuality as that of Homer Watson. Is not the beautiful pastoral tract of western Ontario, which Watson interprets, as much a part of Canada as Algonquin Park?" Charlesworth was right; but by that time Watson was painting landscapes that borrowed ideas from the Group of Seven.

One of the strongest bonds between Watson, Walker, and most other landscape painters of their era was that they tended to paint as much for their customers as for themselves; the style they sought was the popular one. Salesmanship worked better for Walker than it did for Watson, who died bankrupt in the 1930s. Walker's talent had been precocious. He earned his first fee in his teens when the Orangemen in his home town gave him twenty dollars to paint King Billy on his white horse. On the day of the parade he swaggered uptown and blew his friends to everything twenty dollars would buy, including the shave-shampoo-and-hair-cut treatment at the local Negro barbershop. For the rest of his life Walker dramatized everything he painted, and eventually his popularity outpaced Watson's and most other North American painters'. When the St. Louis Art Museum bought a painting called *Wood Cutters* from him in 1906 the price—ten thousand dollars—was said to be the highest yet paid a native artist on this continent. He died within two years of Watson, but in comfort.

The same popular vein was worked by several other artists of the era—men like William Brymner, Frederick Bell-Smith and Franklin Brownell—and at least one, George Reid, had almost as much success in the marketplace. Reid was the third of an Ontario farmer's nine children, and took a thrashing whenever his father caught him frittering away his time with crayons and paper. An hour's privacy was a painfully won luxury for young Reid, which is why his painting of a boy reading in a hayloft (page 56) is called *Forbidden Fruit*. Later, when he was wandering the Ontario back country on sketching expeditions, Reid claimed to have lived a story that is more often heard as a not-very-funny joke. Caught far from a town with a rough night coming on he asked a farmer for supper and a bed. The farmer asked him what he could do to pay for them. Reid said he was a painter, and the farmer told him to paint the end of the barn. Reid did an oil sketch of the barn's end in his usual romanticized style and then, he later said, managed to pacify the angry farmer by telling him the sketch was worth twenty-five dollars if he wanted to sell it. Whether or not

a Reid sketch was worth that much at the time, it certainly was later. Reid went on to become president of the RCA on the strength of some of the most popular paintings of his time under titles like *Foreclosing the Mortgage*. Like Walker, he prospered.

While the fashionable artists of the day were turning out popular pictures in Toronto, the first and in many ways the most dedicated of the Canadians who have painted for painting's sake alone was growing up in Montreal. Maurice Cullen, who was born in St. John's, Newfoundland, in 1866, became in a quiet way the strongest native influence on later Canadian painters. He had first wanted to be a sculptor, and as an apprentice he helped put up the great figures of the apostles by Louis-Philippe Hébert that still dominate the roofline of St. James Cathedral in downtown Montreal. But he soon turned to painting and in Paris, where he went to study, achieved the remarkable distinction of election to the Société Nationale des Beaux Arts at twenty-six, thereby joining a circle of painters that included Whistler and Degas. The French government bought one of his paintings and an important critic offered to help him sell more, but there was a bond that made Cullen choose Canada—probably against his own best interest.

Cullen settled down to paint in Montreal. He had learned a great deal from the Impressionists in France, although he had not become one of them, and he was the first to pass on their insights and methods to painters who had never been outside Canada. Cullen "strove while mixing a tone on the palette," his friend Robert Pilot wrote, "to keep the colours as separate as possible so that liveliness and vibrancy would be achieved." He was a meticulous craftsman who prepared his own canvases and panels, ground his own colours and even carved and gilded his own frames. His paintings were almost all quiet, closely observed studies of nature. But this was the beginning of the gilded era at the turn of the century, and Canadians who had been taught to look for more opulent pictures in the salons of Toronto paid little attention to Cullen. He was made an official war artist in 1918 but long before that he had become a private hero to many younger Canadian painters, particularly some of the members of the Group of Seven. Once, looking at Cullen's *Logging in Winter* (page 17), Arthur Lismer turned to a friend and said that it was Cullen who had taught him how to paint snow. This and other tributes passed from one painter to another were Cullen's chief reward for a lifetime of painting in Canada, a barren history that contrasts painfully with the story of Cullen's friend J. W. Morrice, an equally gifted painter who chose to stay away from Canada. Morrice was a law student and spare-time painter when William Van Horne, the CPR's construction boss, saw one of his canvases. He bought the painting and persuaded Morrice's father to let him pay his son's fare to France to study painting. Morrice, a small, bald, eccentric man who lived alone most of his life, quickly became one of the established figures of European painting. The English novelist Arnold Bennett used him as the model for the artist-hero of *Buried Alive*, and Somerset Maugham used him in the same way in *Of Human Bondage*. By 1907 an eminent French critic wrote that since the death of Whistler, Morrice was the first North American painter to have achieved in Paris a great and well-merited place in the world of art. Matisse called him "the artist with the delicate eye," perhaps in tribute to the subtle rose glow that he was the first to discover in the undersides of grey clouds. In his later years he returned less and less to Canada. "What the hell is the matter with them in Montreal?" he asked in the 1920s. "Why don't they buy modern painting?" He may have been speaking of himself, but more likely he was thinking of his friend Maurice Cullen, of whom he had said, "He's the man in Canada who gets at the guts of things." Cullen died almost unnoticed in Canada; when Morrice died in Paris the Autumn Salon that year was turned over to a

retrospective exhibition of his works, an honour accorded only a few foreign artists in this century.

Morrice and Cullen were still alive, though, when the future of Canadian painting began to take a different turn in Toronto. Once again, the first push came from commercial art. At the old graphic arts firm called Grip, Ltd., which had once published Canada's liveliest satirical magazine, a designer named J. E. H. MacDonald and a younger man named Tom Thomson, a letterer and commercial designer, began trying to work out together some of the problems of painting in Canada. When their art director moved to a competing firm, Rous and Mann, they followed; before long this studio had recruited Franz Johnston, a local painter, two English immigrants, Arthur Lismer and Fred Varley, and finally another Canadian, Franklin Carmichael. Meanwhile Lawren Harris, whose family was better known for making farm machinery, had returned from studying art in Europe. The seven painters formed a close circle; a little later they drew in an eighth member, A. Y. Jackson, and for the time being the group was complete.

What were they looking for? First of all, a solution to the old three-forked dilemma of Canadian painting: to paint in a popular but outworn and irrelevant European style just because it sold, or to be ignored like Cullen, or to leave the country like Morrice. They set out to establish a Canadian school of painting that was original in both content and style; they were as nationalistic as any politician, and they knew it. "You have only to look over the catalogues of (Canadian) exhibitions and you see trails crawling all over Europe," Jackson wrote a friend. "Ye Gods, imagine Monet pottering around Jamaica, Pissaro hard at it in Japan, Renoir out in the Rockies—and the French Impressionists would never have existed." This was a fate they were determined to avoid for their as-yet undeveloped Canadian National Style, and so they remained in a tight group, working out their ideas together, criticizing each other's paintings, going north together whenever they could on sketching expeditions. The romantic, restless spirit of Tom Thomson turned them toward the unpainted wastes of the Laurentian Shield, and that was where they found the Canada they had been looking for. "You could feel yourself," one of them said, "standing on the backbone of the world."

The war held off their first group exhibition. Jackson, Varley, Lismer, Johnston and Harris did war work or helped paint Canada's part in the struggle. While they were away Thomson drowned in an unexplained canoe accident. They were saddened but not stopped; by 1919 they were back in the bush. All that fall they explored to the north of Georgian Bay and Lake Superior, working out of an Algoma Central Railway boxcar that was hauled a few miles up the track every second day by a passing freight train. The next year they had their first exhibition, and for the first time were called the Group of Seven.

Their paintings were instantly denounced as daubs and hot mush; as the products of deranged minds; as drunken figments, bad dreams, and all the other abusive phrases that are dusted off once in every artistic generation by the supporters of the last one. (One of the Group of Seven's most original contributions to art was a modern weapon for striking back. When they came upon a new but ugly feature of the northern landscape, they named it after the angriest of their critics. That is how Charlesworth Swamp appeared on their map of Canada, and another depressing body of water called Telegram Lake, after the man and the newspaper that led the chorus of complaint against their early shows.)

The first strong critical words in their favour had to be imported. In the paintings they displayed at the Wembley Exhibition

of 1924 the London critics saw the beginnings of a distinctively Canadian style of landscape painting. "Their work was rude, they chopped at their paintings as if they were chopping wood," Wyndham Lewis wrote later. "They adopted often the brutal methods of billboard artists to put their country across, big and harsh and plain: with all its emptiness and savagery." Canadians may have been waiting to be told what was Canadian; in any case, within a few years the "mad, wild" paintings of the Group of Seven had been established as the popular model of what a Canadian painting should be.

They had arrived at the right time. Canada was fresh from proclaiming the national integrity of her troops in World War I, and ready to go to the bargaining table to throw off the last remains of her colonial past. When Jackson said that the Canadian artist had been humble long enough, and that it was time to turn from the old European ways of looking at this new land, he seemed to be saying what the whole country was thinking. By going north— Jackson, Varley and Harris went clear to the shores of the Arctic Ocean and beyond—the artists of the Group grafted themselves to the line of Canadian heroes that runs from the voyageur to the bush pilot. In the city the painters of the Group adopted some of the style and language of athletes. They talked about "roughing it in the bush. The idea," Arthur Lismer said long afterwards, "was romantic; if you were uncomfortable enough, you could paint a masterpiece." The drowning of Tom Thomson, the legendary woodsman, came to be thought of less as a canoe accident than as a destiny he had been called to—the mysterious north claiming her favourite son. There has probably never been a group of painters who caught the popular imagination of their time so completely.

That this was not entirely a good thing for Canadian painting is clear enough forty years later. That they were good painters, and that the freshness of their style and the strength of their colours were welcome, is beyond question. That they established a great school of painting, or even a highly original one, is probably untrue. Their commercial training and their inability to shake off some of the forms of *art nouveau* inhibited their freedom to carry forward the style they had set. (The shapes in Tom Thomson's early panel on page 23 are in the *art nouveau* manner; the same shapes are not hard to find in A. Y. Jackson's *Red Maple* on page 21.) Despite what Wyndham Lewis had said, their north was a stylized wilderness, and the non-commercial ideas they used in their paintings came down to them from the Impressionists and Expressionists of Europe. This is natural enough; the trouble was that for a generation or two the mill-run of Canadian painters copied their style as assiduously as the Roman sculptors copied the Greeks, and most Canadian painting became a bush-league bore.

The best Canadian painting of the 1930s was done by isolated

Tom Thomson
*Decorative Panel* / n.d.   oil on board   47¹/₂ x 38
National Gallery of Canada

**23**

Carl Schaefer
*Farm House by the Railway*
1938-9    oil    34 x 46
Art Gallery of Hamilton

individuals who shared their ideas and, indeed, their lives with almost no one. Three of them, superb painters who each in his own way has a claim to genius, are treated in some detail in Chapter Seven: David Milne, Emily Carr, and the great recluse who had long before emerged from the Roman Catholic tradition of Quebec, Ozias Leduc. A few painters did manage to stay in the mainstream of Canadian painting, where critical taste and judgment were now completely dominated by the Group of Seven style, and still get something of themselves into their work. One of them was Carl Schaefer, who painted southern Ontario under the blight of the depression with bitter, staccato strokes of his brush. In a curious way, Schaefer brought back to Canadian painting an interest in people. "The human figure is absent," a critic wrote of Schaefer's work, "but it is present by implication. Man has been there and will be there again." What he meant becomes clearer after a look at Schaefer's *Farm House by the Railway* (right).

Jack Nichols
*Troops in Hospital*
1946    oil on canvas    54 x 40½
National Gallery of Canada

Schaefer became an official RCAF artist in World War II. By then there were several younger artists whose main interest was people, painters like Jack Nichols who had left school during the depression at fourteen and was used to working seventy-five hours a week for a five-dollar bill. The National Gallery assigned Nichols, who was largely self-taught, to paint life in the merchant navy and later the RCN. Men shoehorned between decks in common discomfort and danger were a natural subject for a chronicler of the human condition like Nichols, and there is in his war paintings (right) a compassion that is not common in Canadian painting.

While Nichols was painting at sea, the war was causing the first stirring of a great renewal in French-Canadian painting. With Paris about to fall, Alfred Pellan came home from France and, according to another important Quebec painter, Jacques de Tonnancour, supplied "the blow from the outside that resurrected French-Canadian art from its lethargy." Pellan was a locomotive engineer's son who had escaped from the grim district of Quebec City where he grew up by selling the National Gallery a painting at sixteen and leaving soon after for France on a special scholarship. By 1937, when he won the grand award in the first salon of mural art in Paris, he was an important and exciting figure, and his return to Montreal blew hot new ideas down the cold corridors of Quebec art. A second superb French-Canadian painter of Pellan's generation, Paul-Emile Borduas, put this ferment into words in a manifesto signed by fifteen of Quebec's young painters (including Jean-Paul Riopelle, a younger associate of Borduas's who was later to become the most famous expatriate of *his* generation). The manifesto was called *Refus Global*, and it called on Quebec's artists "to break finally with all the conventional patterns of society; to oppose openly its opportunistic spirit . . . refuse to close our eyes to the crimes of society and the confidence tricks perpetrated under the

guise of wisdom. . . . We shall follow joyfully our violent fight for liberation." By now, of course, it is clear that the manifesto was the first shot fired in the campaign that brought down the Union Nationale and unleashed the wave of nationalism that has made many young Quebeckers separatists in the 1960s. But most of the changes, whether they are for better or worse, came too late for Borduas. In the face of almost universal hostility he went into exile, first in New York and then in Paris, where he died in 1960.

Borduas and Pellan both took a great deal from the Surrealists, but the use they made of these ideas was completely different. Pellan most often paints a magical scene embellished by real and semi-abstract decorations. At first sight *L'Affût* (page 25), as Donald Buchanan points out, looks like a science fiction nightmare. But look again: the two warring machines are mechanical alley cats. Borduas's paintings, by contrast, tell no story and play no tricks. Their harmony and tension were meant to arise from his subconscious, without plan or even thought. Later, when he had looked at the finished canvas for a while, he wrote a title for it. Of all schools of modern painting, Automatisme (as his style is called) has probably been denounced as an empty fake more often than any other. The denunciation is hard to argue with; but so is the musical clarity of many of Borduas's paintings. *Epanouissement* (opposite) is, quite plainly, beautiful.

The ideas that dragged the art world of Montreal kicking and screaming into the twentieth century when Pellan came back from France took longer to penetrate Canada as far as Toronto. But here and there a single English-speaking painter struggled with them. The only important—and the most interesting—of these lonely men was Jock Macdonald, who had come to Canada from Scotland during the first success of the Group of Seven. Like everyone else, Macdonald tried their style for a while. But during the next thirty years he worked his way through most of the other styles that, together, are called "modern" painting: he painted abstracts, symbolic paintings, "touch" paintings, surrealist paintings, automatic paintings, and, finally, the kind of "pure feeling" paintings called abstract expressionist. By this time the vitality of the abstract expressionists in New York had shifted the world capital of painting from Paris to America, and when Macdonald showed some accomplished canvases in this style during the early 1950s there were several younger artists eager to follow his lead.

They began staging group shows under the name Painters Eleven. Although the group was not particularly close and lasted only a few years (Macdonald died, probably of overwork, in 1960), their exhibitions marked as clearly as anything did the final turning point in the first hundred years of Canadian painting—the next major shift will have to come during the second century. Since the Group of Seven, English-speaking painters in Canada had been trapped by a national style. Painters Eleven gave it up. Now "the language is international but the accent is Canadian," one of the eleven, Harold Town, wrote in the catalogue for an early Painters Eleven show. Town himself embodies the point he made. He began as a commercial artist, and sold no fine art until he was thirty. He has lived in Toronto all his life and has never been out of the city for more than a few weeks at a time. Although he has tried most of the styles of modern art he has never settled for long on one; he evades categories. He has drawn on the methods and theories of artists in periods as remote as the Babylonian and as recent as the day before yesterday, and this, together with his rooted place in the streets of the city where he was born, is probably what makes him the most thoroughly Canadian painter of his time. He is original enough to be unafraid of his own tradition. Like many of his

oils, *The Great Divide* (page 49) can be regarded as a landscape painting. Just as Town works in A. Y. Jackson's studio in the Group of Seven's old Studio Building, much of his painting is infused with the spirit of their work.

During the late 1950s and early 1960s there were some signs that Canadian painters might be entering a golden age of sorts. A new and vital group of painters began to emerge in the west: the Regina Five, led at first by Ronald Bloore (also director of the Norman Mackenzie Art Gallery), Kenneth Lochhead, Arthur McKay, Douglas Morton and Ted Godwin. They were given a full-scale National Gallery exhibition in 1962. The British painter William Townsend, who toured Canada in 1965 as sole juror for the Sixth

Douglas Morton
*Fractured Black*
1963   acrylic on canvas   68 x 47¹/₂
Vancouver Art Gallery

Harold Town
*Great Seal* / 1961   oil on canvas   74 x 82¹/₄
Mr. and Mrs. Percy Waxer, Toronto

Biennial of Canadian Art, said of the prairie group, "The remarkable outburst of painting there is one of the significant events in Canadian art since the *Refus Global*."

By 1960 there were far more young painters doing good work in Canada than there had ever been before. One reason was that they were getting higher prices from more buyers than Canadian painters had for generations, and so were better able to fulfil the demands of professionalism. The market had been carefully cultivated by a group of new gallery operators, of whom the outstanding ones were Avrom Isaacs, Dorothy Cameron, Jerrold Morris and Walter Moos in Toronto, and Camille Hébert in Montreal. (It was at these Toronto galleries, interestingly, that most of the new French-Canadian artists made their names and found the market that allowed *them* to become professionals.) By 1965, though, some of the new galleries were dipping into the red and some of the best, like Miss Cameron's and Hébert's, had closed. The nearest anyone could come to a convincing explanation of the reversal was that the wealthy new collectors who had rushed into the market in the late 1950s had simply filled their walls, and that the new enthusiasm for art had been overestimated.

Whatever the reason, this setback in the marketplace spread less gloom among painters than it would have a generation before.

In the meantime the federal government had become an important patron, both through the Canada Council and the Department of Transport. Architects, too, had turned to the country's painters to help them strike a human note in the public rooms of the monumental office buildings that were spiking up everywhere through the nineteenth-century skyline of urban Canada. The established painters, at least, were more prosperous than they had ever been. A generation before, Harold Town might have been pushed into a rural slum, like David Milne, or out of the country, like Borduas; in 1965 he was a painter with an income tax problem.

But to younger, less solidly established painters Canada was beginning to take on once again the feeling of a cold and comfortless outpost. This time, instead of turning to Europe they were drawn to New York. Michael Snow, the second brilliant talent of Town's generation but Town's polar opposite in temperament and intellect, moved to New York in 1962. Snow's temperament is very close to the ideal of much international art theory in the 1960s— cool rather than hot, classic rather than romantic. For a while he made his living playing the piano—jazz—and in New York his painting has concentrated on a single shape, a "Walking Woman" whose figure he has used to explore the modern environment. He has used the Walking Woman in experimental films and pasted

Michael Snow
*Mixed Feelings*
1965
polymer and enamel on canvas
101 x 61
Courtesy of The Isaacs Gallery,
Toronto

scores of Walking Woman cutouts on signboards in the New York subway system. He went back to look at one of these figures one day, and found a note scrawled on it: "Hi, Mike. I tried to look you up when I was in New York. Couldn't find you."

But the stranger to New York did find the Walking Woman, and his note did find Snow. This story may well point the turn Canadian art, and indeed all art, has taken in our day. The era of the painting that was meant to be a national propaganda poster seems to be gone. Whether the painter is Harold Town in Toronto or Michael Snow in New York or Jean-Paul Riopelle in Paris, the language *is* international; only the accent is local.

# Landscape

Long before all three were great figures in Canadian art, Lismer and Jackson tried to talk Varley into coming north with them instead of staying in the city to paint faces and figures. They told him, in the words of a biographer, that "the main and truly Canadian subject was . . . the land." Varley went. He never became a complete convert in his own painting, but he recognized the truth of what they said for Canadian painting in general. From the beginning, the great question in Canadian painting was never what to paint, but how. The land was always there, the biggest fact in sight. The problem, easy to state but hard to solve, was how to see it for what it really was: something new in the world.

For the first half, more or less, of Canada's first century, the painters working here failed to find a way of their own to see the Canadian landscape. They looked at Canada in precisely the same way that European painters had been looking at France, Holland or England a couple of generations earlier. Photography and democracy, which overran Europe almost simultaneously toward the middle of the nineteenth century, had seemed to create their own demand for a new style of painting. The painters of the time had responded with realistic – which meant photograph-like – "studies" of normal people in their natural surroundings. With regional variations (the Barbizon School in France, the Dutch Landscape School in Holland, the followers of Constable in England) these solid middle-class paintings all looked much alike. They were idyllically natural but careful, and, in a way, moralistic. (They argued the virtues of a life close to the soil. Indeed, they were often painted in earth tones overlaid with heavy varnish, and these specimens still give off the mellow tone of good, rich humus.) From 1880, when the Royal Canadian Academy was formed, until the end of World War I, this was the style of the O'Briens and the Frasers, the Bell-Smiths and the Watsons and the Walkers – the dominant style of Canadian painting.

Years before, in Europe, the painters who followed Manet to Impressionism or Van Gogh to Expressionism had realized that the eye is no camera and the mind no emulsified glass plate. By the 1860s they had begun to paint light and colour rather than objects; or to try to translate sights into the emotional response of the man who sees them. This is what many painters are still trying to do, of course, but it took Canadian painters thirty years to begin. Toward the turn of the century Maurice Cullen, for one, began looking at the Quebec landscape this way. But it wasn't until the Toronto painters who became famous as the Group of Seven splashed their rough gobs of paint in front of the country's eyes that most Canadians realized there really *was* a way to see Canada without depending on imported taste and a vision formed an ocean away.

Although the Group's style was their own they had assembled it from borrowed sources – mainly commercial art, French and Scandinavian painters. Their real genius was geographical: Go North! Their original idea was stunningly simple: To see the land in a new way, paint a country other painters have never seen. (Fraser, Bell-Smith and the rest had painted the Rockies. Their mountains had the lived-in look of civil Alpine landscapes. But where was the old-world model for the scragged jack-pines and bony old rock of the Shield? Nowhere, by God.) Of Algonquin Park, Jackson said: "In Autumn it flamed with red and gold, in winter it wrapped itself in a blanket of dazzling snow, and in springtime it roared with running waters and surged with new life. So why stick to the barnyard, why paint cows and sheep and rural tranquillity?"

So they went north, and though there may have been better Canadian painters before and since, that was the great moment of Canadian painting, the real discovery. After World War II, lagging not quite so far behind painters elsewhere this time, younger men began experimenting with newer ways of seeing, and feeling what they saw. Often these painters leave no recognizable shapes on the canvas, only paint contrasting or harmonizing with more paint. This describes the final paintings in this section, by Harold Town and Kazuo Nakamura. Both paintings are landscapes; both painters are still looking for their own way to see Canada.

Lucius R. O'Brien
*Sunrise on the Saguenay*
1880   oil on canvas   34½ x 49½
National Gallery of Canada

## An engineer's mind guiding a painter's hand and eye

Until he turned forty Lucius O'Brien was a practical man, first articled to an architect and then trained to practise as a civil engineer. When he finally took up painting, in 1872, his eye was for economic fact as well as poetic image. A critic later said of his painting *Kakabeka Falls*, "It gives full evidence that this engineer-turned-artist was aware of the geographical and geological features of the terrain: the rock structure, the contours of the land, the kinds of timber. It was almost as if he were compiling a document that would be valuable to those interested in the economic development of the Lakehead district." Most of O'Brien's paintings have the same stamp; under the misty oils of his painting of Cape Trinity (above) there is a surveyor's plan of the bay and the bluffs. When the directors of the CPR looked for painters to send west through the unseen and unexploited country, he was the ideal man. For the same reason, he was the logical candidate when George Grant chose an art editor for *Picturesque Canada*, an encyclopaedic collection of prose and wood engravings copied from paintings and sketches. (The book turned out to be a gallant but futile attempt by the hand craftsmen of the time to stand off the day of photo-mechanical picture reproduction.) For all his late start, O'Brien became the most solidly entrenched member of the Canadian art establishment as it began to take shape in the 1880s. He was the first president of the Royal Canadian Academy and a vice-president of the Ontario Society of Artists; he painted in Windsor Castle and Buckingham Palace by order of Queen Victoria herself. He had come full circle: his father had been an English lieutenant-colonel whom a visitor to the O'Brien house on Lake Simcoe had called "evidently a thorough gentleman."

33

Homer Watson
*The Mill Ford* / 1898   oil on canvas on board   34 x 48
Art Gallery of Hamilton

## A man in love with a valley and its people

The Grand River rises not far from Georgian Bay and loops south to Lake Erie through the heart of the southern Ontario peninsula, the boskiest reach of Canada by far. On the Grand, at a village called Doon, Homer Watson was born in 1855. By painting the Grand and the life that went on around it he became Canada's boskiest and, for a while, most honoured painter. Two of his earliest entries to the Royal Canadian Academy were bought for Queen Victoria and now hang in Windsor Castle. He was the first president of the Canadian Art Club, and was later elected president of the RCA itself. Like his contemporary Horatio Walker (page 15), Watson was a child prodigy; at eleven he drew a creditable sketch of the Battle of Ridgeway, the stirring engagement fought that year against the Fenian raiders. Today Watson seems to have been the kind of painter who never ventured far from the theme and style that had won him his first popularity. In his own day, though, Watson argued the contrary case: his purpose, he said, was to do "something beautiful irrespective of popularity or selling qualities." The "so-called modern paintings," he said later, "are nothing more than advertising posters."

## A time for boldness

There was in John William Beatty's painting (right) and in his life much of the drive for boldness and action that were the hallmarks of the Group of Seven when they came to establish a national style of painting for Canada. As a boy of sixteen Beatty marched with the expedition that put down the second Riel uprising in 1885. Back home in Toronto he got a job as a fireman, and his trick of diving down the brass pole head first made him a minor local celebrity even before he started to paint. He eventually became head of the art department at the Ontario College of Art, but he remained a brash man. "In twenty years," he said after World War I, "Canadian art will lead the world."

Clarence A. Gagnon
*The Wayside Cross, Autumn* / n.d.   oil on canvas   20¼ x 28¼
National Gallery of Canada

## A place for caution

Unlike Beatty (above) Clarence Gagnon avoided boldness, or indeed the risk of trying anything new, all his life. His style was the careful, traditional one of the academies in Montreal and Paris where he studied at the turn of the century, and his subjects were the safely picturesque habitants of Quebec. But within these limits he was a highly accomplished craftsman. The wayside cross (right) is as meticulously drawn as the details of the nearby houses and the panorama beyond. Gagnon's best-known works are his etchings, and the colour illustrations for the famous novel of frontier life, *Maria Chapdelaine.*

John Fraser
*Lake Scugog* / 1873   oil on canvas   16 x 30
National Gallery of Canada

## Not just seeing it, but liking it

Duck hunters who make the short trek to Lake Scugog, twenty miles north of Oshawa, can still find patches of lakefront unimproved by bulldozers. For those who do the scene at dusk is the same one John Fraser painted in 1873. The surprises that Fraser sprang on his public during his lifetime have continued since his death. He made his first mark by hand-painting miniature photographs, then became even better known for his huge mist-shrouded panoramas of the Rockies (see page 10). Between them he painted the lively canvas at the left, which was lost until recently. When it turned up, art historians scrambled to reassess Fraser's talent. This painting is probably the first Canadian landscape that is unmarked by deference to European taste. Fraser liked what he saw at Lake Scugog, and painted it with gusto; one critic calls it gorgeous. Fraser was praised while he was alive, particularly by the young painters he led in organizing the Ontario Society of Artists, but he was also disliked in many quarters. He appraised his own ability highly, and art reviews of the time often dwell at greater length on Fraser's arrogance than they do on the quality of his art.

Albert H. Robinson
*Baie St. Paul* / n.d.   oil on wood panel   11 x 13
Art Gallery of Toronto

## The first signs of a bolder, rougher look

Although Albert Robinson was never a member of the Group of Seven he was close to several of them, particularly A. Y. Jackson, and paintings like the one above are clearly very close to their style. Robinson was a born painter. When the principal of his Hamilton public school gave him a one-month suspension for passing notes, they were illustrated notes. When he dropped out of school to go to work, it was in the art department of the Hamilton *Times* for five dollars a week, and when they gave him a raise to nine, he saved enough to quit *that* and go to Paris to study painting. As a mature painter he did most of his work in and around Montreal, where a patron gave him a rent-free studio. In time he came to share many of the ideas that were developed by such Quebec painters as Cullen and Gagnon. In Toronto, Jackson said he learned a lot from Robinson, as Robinson undoubtedly did from him. They were both, from time to time, among the painters who forgathered in Baie St. Paul, downriver from Quebec City, at the invitation of a local hotelman who let them set their own rates. This accounts for the large number of Baie St. Paul townscapes in Canadian art collections.

## Building the Canadian heritage and legend

This is the look and feel of the Canadian land that the Group of Seven gave us, and that the rest of the world accepted as an accurate account of what it is really like here. Arthur Lismer was barely off the boat from England when he took a job at the commercial studio in Toronto where the nucleus of the Group was forming, but he was peculiarly open to the kind of country he found; he is now part of the Canadian heritage and legend. His paintings are as powerful as any done by the Group – taut, economical, built from strong shapes and colours. "I think the Chinese have the right idea," Lismer once wrote, "that nature is man and not merely his background – things in nature are alive with man's intention, adoration and praise – they become the measure of his stature and worship." Of which his friend Lawren Harris said, "If we view his paintings with this statement in mind, we will find that they are great human documents." Lismer is the only living member of the Group who went on to become a great teacher, possibly one of the greatest living teachers of painting to young children. His classes are in Montreal, but his methods are used in most of the English-speaking countries, Italy and Belgium.

Tom Thomson
*Moose at Night* / n.d.  oil on panel  8¹/₂ x 10¹/₂
National Gallery of Canada

## Stalking the moods of the north like a hunter

Tom Thomson was three years dead by drowning when the Group of Seven was named in 1920, but if the Group had a spirit of its own at the beginning, it was Thomson's. He met them over the drawing board in Toronto, but he led them to Algonquin Park, where he was a denizen of the bush in the same way that the moose at the top of this page were. "I've been with him in the woods," Arthur Lismer said in 1953, "when I've got the definite feeling that he was part of them, when the birds and animals recognized something in him that they had themselves. That's why I say that the rest of us were painting pictures; he was expressing moods. He was simply a part of nature." Thomson had grown up on a farm near Owen Sound on Georgian Bay, on the rough lower lip of the Shield, and did nearly all his paintings—three hundred of them—in the same ragged, burned-over part of Algonquin Park that the moose are passing through above. He stalked the moods of the raw land like a hunter. He once asked a ranger where he could find three spruce trees, black, cold and ragged against a north sky. The ranger told him. It was three days before Thomson came back. He had waited for the right light.

J. E. H. MacDonald
*Leaves in The Brook* / 1919   oil on canvas   21 x 26
McMichael Conservation Collection of Art, Kleinburg, Ontario

## Painting the inner life of a plant, a rock, or a stream

When the future members of the Group of Seven began arriving in Toronto before World War I, they found J. E. H. MacDonald already there, his first one-man show of painting freshly behind him. Mac-Donald was in charge of design at the Grip studio; when he quit to become a free-lance artist, he had been a professional designer for sixteen years. This may very well be what determined the most

prominent characteristic of the National Style the Group was already beginning to develop — the massing and simplifying of shapes and colours that are the trademark of a good commercial designer. From Thomson on, the young painters around him learned much about design from MacDonald. When he talked or wrote about painting, he framed an argument the reverse of the one that domin-

ates art in the 1960s. Art should "join us all equally in the contemplation of something larger than our little selves," he said; an artist trying to express nothing more than himself was wasting his time. The "larger" vision MacDonald spent his life trying to capture was the "inner life" of nature. He painted it in Toronto, in Algoma, in the Rockies. He painted it well, and at times he painted it with glory.

A. Y. Jackson
*Grey Day, Laurentians* / 1922   oil on canvas   21 x 26
McMichael Conservation Collection of Art, Kleinburg, Ontario

## Taking to the woods for kicks — and images

For Socrates' *know yourself* the Group of Seven substituted *know the land.* Between 1919 and 1929 A. Y. Jackson painted large stretches of Algoma, the lower St. Lawrence, the B. C. mountains, the barrenlands and the high arctic. In 1927 he wrote the *Mail and Empire* in Toronto, "If we could import a few Mimis and Yvonnes to cheer up our dull studios with their gay laughter and songs while they in-

spired us with their beautiful poses, we might create an art atmosphere here; but failing that we have taken to the woods to get what kicks we can out of lone pine trees, rock and muskeg." The self-derogatory tone (as well as the swipe at Canadian stodginess) was characteristic of Jackson. He valued the warmth of the studio so little that he became known as *Père* Racquette on the lower St.

Lawrence, because he was usually seen slogging through the bush on snowshoes. Jackson's formal art training was relatively broad: Montreal, Paris, Rotterdam, Chicago. His knowledge of colour and the Impressionist analysis of light and shadow were extensive; he passed on a great deal of technical expertise. Later, he introduced the slash and thrust of Expressionist brushwork.

Lawren Harris
*Snow Squalls Pic Island* / 1923   oil on panel   12 x 15
McMichael Conservation Collection of Art, Kleinburg, Ontario

## The search for an art as pure as music

While most of the other members of the Group refined their styles and enlarged their interests after the great success of the 1920s, Lawren Harris was the only one who went all the way with the changing demands of modernism. Harris wrote the Group's manifesto that defined the new National Style. After 1924 he seldom signed or dated the painting he was working on at the time, convinced that the ideal painting was impersonal and universal. The drive of his ideas led him to abstract paintings and by 1954 he was writing in defence of Abstract Expressionism, then a recent and widely ridiculed innovation. Harris had been, all along, the intellectual member of the National movement. He read deeply in philosophy, from Plato to the Upanishads, and sought in the pale and open arctic a spiritual climate that might enable Canadians to achieve "a more certain conviction of eternal values" in their art. He made a long arctic voyage in 1930, and wrote of it: "We are on the fringe of the great north and its living whiteness . . . its resignation and release, its call and answer, its cleansing rhythms." Since 1942 his painting has all been abstract; he is looking for an art as pure as music.

Jacques de Tonnancour
*Paysage de Juin* / 1957   oil on canvas   31¹/₄ x 43³/₄
National Gallery of Canada

## A sea of silence

Compared to almost all other living painters in Canada or anywhere else, Jacques de Tonnancour has moved ahead in the last ten years by going backward. Twenty years ago de Tonnancour was already a well-known, accomplished figure painter. Like most other painters, he then turned to abstraction, and by 1950 he was regarded as one of Quebec's most promising abstract painters. That year he quit painting. "My work," he said, "has become very cold and intellectual." Five years later he was ready to paint again; but he had backed up from abstracts all the way to landscapes as literal as the one on these pages. He has concentrated on landscapes ever since, mainly of northern Quebec. "The magnetic and engulfing charm and power of the north can in no time dissolve a man and lose him in a sea of silence and desolation," he said in 1959. "In many parts of Canada that is what we are up against, that enormous silence. This is the shape of it in Quebec." His words might have been an afterthought by the Group of Seven but his paintings could come from a different world, as in a sense they do. Looking at the painting reproduced here is like opening your eyes and taking in the entire scene in an instant. He paints swiftly but lightly, not in masses of paint but in thin washes and the fine skipping strokes of a draughtsman. But if his paintings have a sense of immediacy, he means them to be thought about; he is himself an almost painfully serious artist. "Hope for Canadian art," he has said, ". . . will be an automatic consequence of developing better integrated human beings [with] an insight into eternity."

Frederick Varley
*Landscape with Eskimos, Baffin Island*
1940   water-colour   8³/₄ x 11³/₄
Art Gallery of Toronto

## Humanity and passion

Like the other members of the Group, Frederick Varley ranged Canada like an explorer. He sailed inside the Arctic Circle and brought back over two hundred landscapes and water-colours of Eskimo life (left) for the National Gallery. Earlier he had painted the battle-fields of France during World War I, and his *Some Day the People Will Return* of 1918 is an eloquent protest against war. After the war he packed by foot to Mount Garibaldi with Jock Macdonald. But landscape – "the truly Canadian subject" – was not an obsession with Varley. "Where the Group was romantic Varley was mystic," one critic said. "Where the Group indulged in virile starkness Varley suffered from his . . . humanism."

## Calmness and action

Calm stamps the painting style of Will Ogilvie–oddly, because action has stamped his life. He was born in South Africa, and trained as a painter there and in New York before he came to Canada in 1925. Many of his controlled paintings of World War II engagements were made from sketches drawn in a moving jeep under fire; he waded from a landing barge to the beach in Sicily and into an action that won him the military OBE. Within Canada, his best and most typical paintings have dealt with calm moods of Georgian Bay. A leading geologist who admires both Ogilvie's painting and his powers of observation has remarked that no Canadian artist ever painted rocks better.

J. W. G. (Jock) Macdonald
*Forbidden Valley*
1957   oil on masonite   42 x 48
Mrs. Hugh Mackenzie, Toronto

## Looking into the spirit of the land

In the early 1930s J. W. G. Macdonald and Frederick Varley started the B. C. School of Art. Within two years they lost their money. Varley went east, but Macdonald left for Nootka Sound on Vancouver Island with his wife and daughter. Their campsite was six miles from the village; on the way their small boat capsized. A Russian hermit helped them salvage a few things, but they lost most of what they owned. (The hermit, whose name was Fred, became the basis of a still-current legend about a conversation in the woods between Macdonald and a mysterious woman who spoke of the essences of forms.) The Macdonalds lived at Nootka for a year and a half, at first in a tent and later in a shanty, eating mainly fish that Jock caught from his small boat. The rain forest had a powerful effect on his Celtic imagination. Although *Forbidden Valley* (above) was painted later, its eerie mood and the shapes of the rocks and the cave had been planted in his mind at Nootka. In this painting, Macdonald was about half way between the Group of Seven style of landscape painting and the free, spontaneous compositions of pure colour and light that he was painting in the last two years of his life.

## The landscape from thirty thousand feet

When Harold Town executed two murals for the terminal building at Toronto's airport, he had never been off the ground. In both murals, though, his view of Malton from above is easily recognizable to anybody who has arrived there by air. Then, in 1965, when he was in his early forties, he flew for the first time. He was excited by what he saw happening to perspective at great heights, and *The Great Divide* (opposite page) is one of the results. He seems to have telescoped the view out the window during and at the end of a night flight, a way of seeing the landscape that is becoming a normal one for many Canadians. The resourcefulness needed to compress a sight track several hundred miles long into a single painting is less surprising coming from Town than it might be from a different painter. Town has always been an inventive man. His first studio was in a basement where "the headroom was so limited I used to wear a toque stuffed with Kleenex to break the shock. I wound up wearing a football helmet. A doctor finally ordered me out; I was developing a kind of fungus." At the time, the money he could pick up dressing windows and doing other odd jobs on the fringes of commercial art was too little to support him. He made it up by acting – on radio station CKEY.

Harold Town
*The Great Divide*
1965   oil on canvas   90 x 60
Courtesy of the Artist

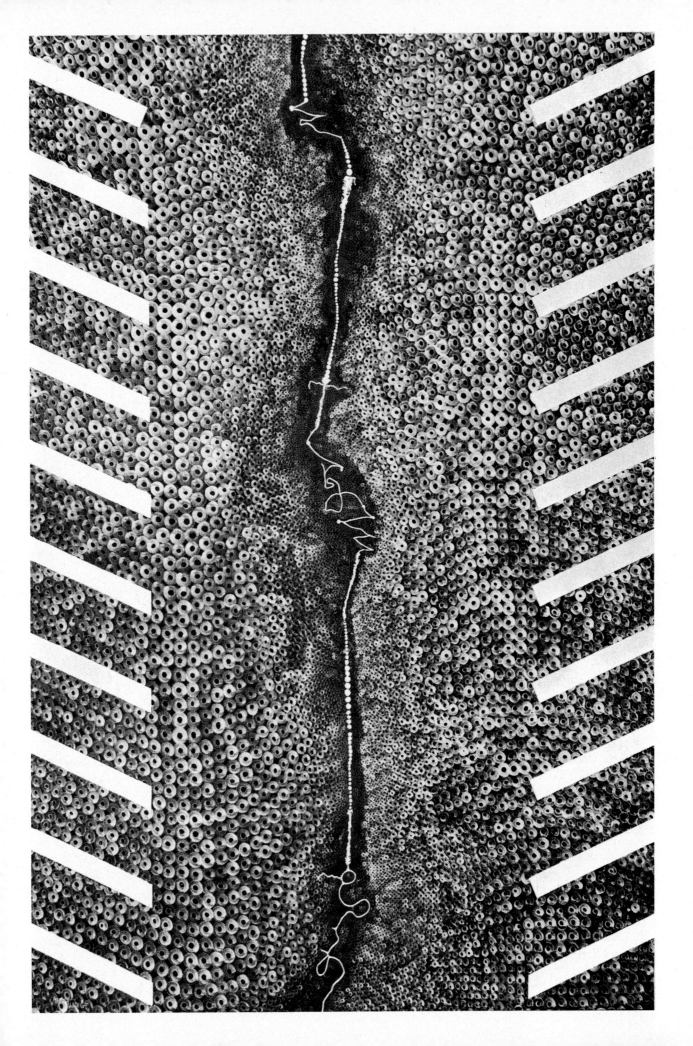

Kazuo Nakamura

*Core Structure* / 1964   oil on canvas   36¹/₂ x 42

Courtesy Jerrold Morris International Gallery, Toronto

## Trying to paint the sense of the land

Kazuo Nakamura was in high school when Canada defended herself by dispersing him and the other Canadians of Japanese origin in Vancouver to a series of work camps in the hinterland. Despite the paranoidal auspices of this introduction to the interior of his country, Nakamura has painted Canada as a civilized, rational country. The arrangement of striations in *Core Structure* (above) looks like prairie grainfields meeting the horizon close to the top of the picture. After a long, close look at the painting, the surface seems to undulate slowly, like a stand of wheat in a steady wind. "These people of Oriental descent are never foolish enough to despise the elements — wind and snow and storm and quiet weather — which are such factors in our view of form in nature," a critic wrote of his early work. Nakamura reduces the landscape to a carefully con-trolled design, but he is after something more. He wants to capture the sense of the land, the feeling it draws from people. When critics speak of him they invariably draw parallels between his painting and Oriental calligraphy, poetry, or aesthetic sense in general. This is probably misleading; Nakamura is an intensely individual artist, and a thoroughly Canadian one. He studied in Toronto, and was a member of Painters Eleven.

# Daily Life

Although landscape has been the great and recurring theme of Canadian painting, there have been others. By dominating the popular imagination so thoroughly, in fact, landscape painting may have obscured more interesting, accomplished Canadian paintings than it has thrown into the public eye. The next three sections of this book, on daily life, the cities, and the figures and faces of the people in them, are meant partly to help break the fixation on the empty land that has given Canadian painting its single-eyed image for so long.

Paintings of people going about their everyday affairs are usually called genre paintings. The way the word is used often makes the paintings it describes sound, somehow, less serious and valuable than, say, still-lifes or nudes, but there is no convincing reason for this. Rembrandt painted genre; so did most of the Canadian painters who have become our cultural celebrities. Krieghoff's paintings, for a start, were genre more often than not. He tended to set the scene more theatrically than the realities of the Laurentian bush may have justified, and to move his characters around a little like a stage-manager setting up a puppet show for the pleasure of a childish audience. But the details of his habitants' houses, inside and out, their sleighs, the clothes they wore, the card games they played and the pots and pans they used to cook in, are an irreplaceable visual record of their region and time. They have become an exuberant part of our heritage, and we are lucky to have them.

Krieghoff's gaiety soon gave way to the mellifluous realism described at some length in the introduction to the previous chapter. The curious thing about this school, which again documented fairly carefully the working day of ordinary people, particularly farm labourers, was that for all its self-proclaimed "truth to nature" it saw people and places through a far more idealized, romantic haze than old Krieghoff, for all his jollity, would have allowed himself. Frederick Verner's Indian campsite (page 58) has that "noble red man" gloss over it; Horatio Walker's farmer (page 59) is part of a highly pleasing picture, but he has the look of a man who has never seen a killing frost or felt his belly shrink in the winter, both fairly common events on the Ile d'Orléans of Walker's time.

At almost the same time, though, this pretty, imported style was being reworked into a harder kind of reporting that became known as the North American realist tradition. George Reid and Robert Harris (pages 56 and 57) were among the strongest painters this tradition produced anywhere on the continent. The character and flavour of Protestant rural Ontario in the 1880s is clearly and powerfully told in Harris's plain, truthful picture of the young teacher confronting the school trustees, from the stuff of their clothes and the shapes of their hands to the expressions on their Calvinist faces. Harris had been there, and you hardly need to see his initials carved into the desk to know it (page 13).

Before Harris died the time of man's willing belief in the essential dignity of man was ending. The big wars came. Canadians, like almost everybody else, left the lonely land to herd in the swelling cities. Often, particularly if they had the raw nerve-ends that are part of a painter's sensibility, they became lonelier the tighter they were wedged into the crowd. The painters of our own time look back with nostalgia, like Louis de Niverville and Jan Wyers, or around them with irony, like William Kurelek and Jean-Paul Lemieux. The old gaiety is gone, and while the people in these new paintings are still drawn with compassion, it now looks less like the shared warmth of love than the shared chill of loneliness, or fear.

In 1965 a Toronto gallery assembled an exhibition mainly composed of pictures dealing with the act of love. Or, as the indictment called it, the sex act; police closed the gallery and the Crown prosecuted its owner in the courts.

## Living a life of gusto—and then painting it

A Dutchman who studied art in Germany and crossed the Atlantic to join the American Army fell in love, instead, with the Venetian-faced daughter of a French-Canadian butcher and baker. In 1841 he moved into her father's house at Longueuil, across the river from Montreal, and began painting the day-to-day lives of her family and their neighbours.

For the next thirty years, Cornelius Krieghoff was both the best-known academic painter and the most accurate visual reporter in Lower Canada. He painted farmers in their kitchens, Colonial officers in their cups, *grandes dames* in their jewels and Indians in their hunting camps. He lived the life he painted, spearing salmon from dugout canoes far upcountry from the settled St. Lawrence valley, and carousing until dawn in the *boîtes* of old Quebec. His gusto is part of his painting style: his people wear brilliant colours and sly smiles. He painted hundreds, possibly thousands, of pictures and sometimes stole from himself. "I had to paint for my living," he said at the end of his life. "That is why I made a good many copies."

The living was often hard. From 1849 to 1853 he was never more than a jump away from the rent collector as he moved around Montreal following the only work he could get, painting signs. Then came years when he could afford such luxuries as a trip to Italy with his family, but at the end the living was hard again. On his last trip to Montreal, in 1871, he spent some of his time on St. James Street, peddling from door to door small, daubed sketches he called pot-boilers. In the 1960s an average price for one of his paintings is five thousand dollars, and some have brought more than thirty thousand.

William Raphael / *Immigrants at Montreal* / 1866   oil on canvas   26½ x 43 / National Gallery of Canada

## What the immigrants saw when they stepped ashore a century ago

This is very probably the most accurate pictorial account available of what it was like to land in Canada from Europe in the years just before Confederation. William Raphael came to Montreal from Russia via New York in 1860; art historians have gone out of their way to call him Canada's first Jewish painter. (He may well be the man at the precise centre of the canvas above, who holds an artist's portfolio and a Jewish ceremonial candelabra.) The building behind the wharfside clearing-house is Bonsecours Church; on the harbour, smoke from a single funnel is beginning to blacken the sails.

Franklin Brownell
*Street Scene*
n.d.   oil on board   13 x 9
National Gallery of Canada

## Downtown in the capital

Franklin Brownell was a Paris-trained New Eng-
lander who became head of the Ottawa School
of Art in 1886. The painting above is a look at
downtown Ottawa before the turn of the century.
This was an unusual subject for Brownell, who
preferred the massive bluffs of the Gatineau country or the farmsteads of the Ottawa valley to the
city's streets. His landscapes usually had a very
low horizon; he might have been called a skyscape
painter. "One is conscious of air that moves but
is unseen," a critic said of them, "of leaves that
tremble and shadows that dissolve." He was
famous for clouds and his sense of colour was
called "happy and harmonious."

G. A. Reid
*Forbidden Fruit* / 1889   oil on canvas   30⁵/₈ x 48
Art Gallery of Hamilton

## Two ways of arriving at the same thing: honest realism

Both paintings on these pages belong to what is now called The North American Realist Tradition. This is a strong, careful, unadorned style established by the American painter Thomas Eakins, and passed on by students who came to study under him in Philadelphia. George Reid (above) went from Ontario to study with Eakins for three years in the early 1880s. Robert Harris (opposite page) was a Prince Edward Islander who studied in Boston, London and Paris. He did not, apparently, ever work directly under Eakins, but his style and discipline are as consistently part of the tradition as are Reid's. The book the boy in the loft has hidden away to read is *The Arabian Nights,* one of the first books forbidden Reid by his own father, an unbending member of southern Ontario's Scotch community. Reid's imagination was easily fired; at sixteen he walked fifty miles to meet an English painter who was staying briefly in the district. Harris had worked as a surveyor before he turned seriously to the study of art. Once his sound, orderly style was set he varied it little for the rest of his life. He was a shy man who painted every day or "felt part of my life was wasted."

Frederick Arthur Verner / *Indian Camp* / 1876   oil on canvas   32¹/₂ x 60 / Art Gallery of Hamilton

Blair Bruce / *The Phantom Hunter* / n.d.   oil on canvas   59¹/₂ x 75¹/₄ / Art Gallery of Hamilton

## Lo, the Indians

With the single exception of Niagara Falls, the best-selling standard subject of the nineteenth-century painters who cultivated the export market in England was the Indian; his costume, weapons, and way of life. Paul Kane was the best known of these painters, but from Krieghoff and the adventurer-painter William Hind on, the demand produced a constant supply from the leading painters of the time. Most of them, like Frederick Verner (left, above) romanticized the Indians in the "Noble Red Man" vein. Verner was born in Ontario, but moved to England in middle age and died in London.

## Expatriate visions

After Blair Bruce left his native Hamilton in 1881 to study in Paris he rarely returned to Canada, but he found that illustrations of Canadian legends (left, below) were popular with European patrons. *The Phantom Hunter* (usually titled, wrongly, *Walker of the Snows*) is based on an Indian legend that a hunter crossing a certain valley after nightfall will see a grey ghost. Blair took the story from a poem by C. D. Shanly:

*Not far into the valley*
*Had I dipped upon my way*
*When a dusky figure joined me*
*In a capuchon of grey,*
*Then the fear-chill gathered in me*
*Like a shroud around me cast,*
*As I sank upon the snowdrift*
*Where the shadow-hunter passed.*

Blair never exhibited in Canada, but his widow gave a collection of his works to the Hamilton Art Gallery.

## A report from the Canadien countryside

During the last half of his long life (he died in 1938 at eighty) Horatio Walker painted mainly the farmers and farm animals of the Ile d'Orléans, where he settled in 1883. The painting above is not a religious allegory, but a more or less straightforward report. Roadside replicas of the Crucifixion in plaster were a normal part of the habitant countryside. Paintings like this were not for local consumption; Walker sent them to New York, where they commanded several thousand dollars each from wealthy collectors who saw in them all the virtues of earth and toil. The critic Hector Charlesworth praised them for "virility" and "cosmic power."

Jean-Paul Lemieux
*Lazare* / 1941    oil on masonite    39³/₄ x 32³/₄
Art Gallery of Toronto

Philip Surrey
*Variation on A Theme by Poussin*
1963   oil on canvas   16 x 24
Art Gallery of Hamilton

## New nails, old wounds

The young man in the shorts, sneakers and brightly striped tee-shirt of the 1950s (right) is lying in the traditional position of Christ lowered from the cross – the *pietà*. The sense of a cruel destiny hangs over most of Philip Surrey's paintings, but the details – from tail fins to hair styles – are close copies of the commonplace objects he uses to make his points. Surrey paints society: "He cannot see the street without the people," a writer once said. (Surrey was for many years photo editor of *Weekend*.)

Alex Colville / *Family and Rainstorm*
1955   tempera on board   22½ x 29½ / National Gallery of Canada

## The inner life of a Quebec village

Lazarus rises (opposite page); believers in miracles bring another body to the graveyard; the torpid congregation takes instruction from *m. le curé*; and on the road outside town the village strongmen fight off intruders dropping in by parachute from the outside world. Jean-Paul Lemieux painted *Lazare* in 1941. His mordant pictorial essay was an early warning of the onslaught against *duplessisme* that was already brewing among French Canada's artists. Lemieux was born in Quebec City in 1904, and has painted and taught there all his adult life. He is a painstaking craftsman who seems to have inherited the spirit of the artisans' guilds of old Quebec. He collects *québecois* carving, silver and folklore; in many of his paintings the history of Quebec comes sharply alive. He once told an interviewer, "I try to convey a remembrance, the feeling of generations."

## An eternal instant

Alex Colville's kind of realism is called magic (see page 96), but in his case the mystery depends on absolute accuracy. The lock on the car door, the bunching of the woman's blouse, the sag of the wet bathing suit – they are all so precise that the eye assumes it has seen them before. In a dream, perhaps.

William Kurelek
*Nativity 1965 — We Find All Kinds of Excuses* / 1965   oil on masonite   47 x 72
Courtesy The Isaacs Gallery Toronto

## Flesh and spirit

As a painter, William Kurelek cannot be classified, but as a man he obviously belongs to one of the oldest classes of all, the religious missionaries. When he was a boy his Ukrainian parents moved from farm to farm on the prairies; when he was a young man studying painting on his own in England, he was converted to Catholicism. Since then the scene of nearly all his paintings has been the prairie farmland, but their subject has been Catholic allegory. The pictorial element in Kurelek's painting is remarkably convincing. ". . . they accomplish what few painters even attempt these days," the critic Robert Fulford wrote of them. "They describe particular people in a particular time and place, and they say (with a conviction no photograph could ever manage): *this* is what it was like." For Kurelek, this seems to be true even of the didactic elements in his paintings. The virgin and the child are *there* among the cattle in every exposed stack of hay where people work or play without regard for the salvation of their eternal souls. Saving a soul is infinitely more important than painting a picture or harvesting a crop. Kurelek once withdrew some of his paintings from an exhibition at the Isaacs Gallery in Toronto because several nudes were to be hung at the same time. He was responsible, he said, "not to provide the occasion for anyone to fall." Kurelek is a meticulous craftsman, and doubles as the master-framer for the Isaacs Gallery. But he manages to live almost in solitude, remaining entirely aloof from the Toronto art community.

Jan G. Wyers
*First Saskatchewan Harvest* / n.d.   oil on board   23¹/₂ x 36
R. L. Bloore, Regina

## A cheerful look at a bygone day

The only style of painting Jan Wyers knows is his own. Wyers was a grown man when he emigrated from Holland to Canada in 1913. During the war he found work as night watchman in an Ontario camp for German prisoners of war, and when he began trying to make pictures a knowledgeable prisoner helped him. After the war Wyers moved to Saskatchewan, where he has been farming ever since. In the winter, when the work is lighter, he paints. He has no theories and no pretensions; painting is a pleasure for him, and his canvases have the richness of tapestry. The figures in them look a little like puppets, but the animals — particularly the horses —

have personalities of their own. Wyers seems to be painting from memory the prairies of an earlier era: harvests, sunsets, winter, men at work. He sometimes uses old photographs or calendars as models. Wyers paints few pictures and sells fewer, but in 1959 the Norman Mackenzie Gallery in Regina bought the largest canvas he has done. The painter Ronald Bloore, who is director of the gallery, compares Wyers with the Impressionists because "he avoids the ugly, the unseemly and the atypical." When the National Gallery assembled an exhibit called Folk Painters of the Canadian West, Wyers was a prominent contributor.

Greg Curnoe
*April, May, London, Toronto, Montreal*
1964   oil and Honda insignia on plywood   96 x 96
Courtesy The David Mirvish Gallery Toronto

## Pop! goes the painting

Pop art is a way of painting that takes comic books seriously and glorifies most of the things that are for sale at supermarkets. In Canada the works closest to pop paintings have been done by Greg Curnoe. Curnoe is an ironist, and he usually seems to be satirizing the pop idea. But there is affection in his paintings too, and nostalgia, not for the distant past, but for experiences as recent as last week, or yesterday. The photographs at the far right identify the man on the new Honda as his friend the artist Robert Markle. Markle is the kind of rebel who wears a black leather outfit and rides the biggest Honda on the market.

Louis de Niverville
*The Red-Checkered Tablecloth* / 1960 oil on canvas 48 x 54
Marjorie Harris, Toronto

## To paint a world as whimsical as this, you have to live there

Like the people in his paintings, Louis de Niverville looks a little like a friendly dwarf, and his house in Toronto is furnished like the lush, unreal background in a de Niverville painting. "Since I've never been taught the basic princi-

ples of shape and colour," he said in 1963, "I have to use my own language . . . happy, comic, sarcastic, a little grotesque." In 1957, when he was twenty-four, de Niverville was "discovered" by the graphics department of the CBC.

Before long shows of his drawings were selling out for over a hundred dollars each, and he could have been the richest artist in Canada before he was thirty. Instead he turned to painting; most of the drawings he does now, he destroys.

# The Cities

The portrait of the artist as an introvert has been repeated so often in fiction and biography that it is hard to think of him as anything but a withdrawn man living a busy inner life and almost no social life at all. As it describes painters, this picture is untrue in at least one important respect. Painters may well be the most garrulous class on earth, as voluble as salesmen and as sociable as society matrons with unmarried daughters. They like to be where things are happening — downtown in the marketplace of ideas and new sights and sounds. Few of them find it easy to stay away from the new shows, or for that matter from their dealers or patrons. Above all, they seek the company of their fellow-artists. By competing and borrowing and stealing, or simply by talking and drinking together they soak up a great deal from the urban environment in which they thrive. For all these reasons painters normally congregate in the cities and some of them seem to spend as much time in exchanges with each other as they do in their studios painting.

There are exceptions, of course, but they tend to prove the rule. Emily Carr, the great west coast recluse, had given up painting when Lawren Harris discovered her work. With encouragement from him and other members of the Group of Seven, she began again and went on to paint many of her strongest pictures. Alex Colville lives in Sackville, N.B., hardly a metropolis, but he has young painters around him as students and makes regular trips to New York. Tom Thomson lived in a shack, but many people have forgotten that his shack stood in midtown Toronto.

Although Canadian painters may have struck out for the back country on painting expeditions more often than painters elsewhere, they have had the same homing instinct for the cities. It would seem safe to suppose, then, that the cities with their striking shapes and human richness would be the prime source of material for the painters who live there. That this is untrue is one of the most striking facts about Canadian painting. The only paintings here that show people in the streets — or anywhere else — are by women, Pegi MacLeod and Molly Bobak. But even with them, the people are mainly there to add variety and movement. Gordon Smith and Michael Snow seem to have regarded the city impersonally, as a set of painter's problems in composition, colour or technique, and to have dealt with them the same way they would have dealt with an abstract problem in visual geometry.

There are few people in this gallery of Canadian city-scapes, and only one or two comments on our history as a city-dwelling people. But there are familiar streets and skylines seen more clearly, and even once or twice more joyfully, than most of us ever see them. That is less than we might have expected from our city-centred painters, but as a painter once said, maybe it's more than our town planners (or the towns that don't know what a planner is) deserve.

## Canada's first painter looks at Canada's first city

Before Maurice Cullen, Canada's landscape painters borrowed their style from stilted, formal Dutch and French painters who had already gone out of fashion in Europe. Cullen was the first to paint the truest pictures he could of the Canada he lived in and loved. Cape Diamond and the Citadel of Quebec, which is visible in the far background of this painting, are probably the most romantic subjects in Canada. But Cullen's picture puts the clotheslines and chimneypots of Quebec's traditional working-class houses in the foreground. He was after the feel and smell of life in a small Quebec town, and from that time to this he was one of the very few to get it. To paint Canada, Cullen also set himself to master a technique for painting snow—not the blank white snow that was popular with art lovers of the time, but the snow Cullen actually saw changing hour by hour from cream to rose and blue to violet. Snow, in fact, was one of the main things he asked from life: "A studio of my own, a shack in the mountains, a garden . . . and a heavy snowfall every winter."

Lawren Harris
*Red House and Yellow Sleigh* / n.d.   oil on board   10½ x 13¼
Art Gallery of Toronto

## A rich man's son with a "socialist's" love for the slums

Between 1910 and 1925 Lawren Harris came back repeatedly to the rundown streets of central Toronto to paint scores of house "portraits" that are still the most eloquent record any artist has left of change in a Canadian city. *Red House and Yellow Sleigh* was painted on Spadina Avenue, now the centre of the garment district, in 1919. Because this and other paintings like it were so clearly sympathetic to the people who lived in this declining district, Harris was described as a "socialist" painter by critics who should have known better, but who may have been confused by the way Harris shared his wealth with other painters. He was a grandson of one of the founders of Massey-Harris Ltd., and ploughed back the profits from a long line of farm tools into helping painters like A. Y. Jackson get started. To Harris, Jackson wrote many years later, "art was almost a mission. He believed that a country that ignored the arts left no record of itself worth preserving."

From the Toronto slums to the islands of the high arctic, Harris spent his life adding to the record left by art.

Lionel LeMoine FitzGerald
*Doc Snider's House* / 1931   oil   29¹/₂ x 33¹/₂
National Gallery of Canada

## A prairie boy whose world was in his own back yard

Doc Snyder was a dentist who lived next door to LeMoine Fitzgerald on Lyle Street in Winnipeg during the 1930s. To paint the view across his back yard to Snyder's house in temperatures well below zero, Fitzgerald built a shelter on runners that he pulled around the yard as he changed his vantage point. Fitzgerald's back yard, as a painter, stretched through Winnipeg to the prairie beyond, but farther than this he almost never went. If the world wanted him, the world came to Winnipeg, as the Group of Seven did when they chose him to replenish their number on the death of J. E. H. MacDonald in 1932. (He was the last new member of the Group; in 1933 they merged themselves into a new organization, the Canadian Group of Painters.)

Fitzgerald's writing, like his painting, had a touch of the poet. As a boy he spent his summers on his grandmother's farm at Snowflake, Manitoba. It was here, he later said, where he learned the moods and colours of "the sloughs with their fringes of willow, and the bluffs of poplar with the light trunks and shimmering leaves . . and always the sky."

71

Adrien Hébert
*St. Henri Station* / 1929   oil on canvas   20 x 30
Art Gallery of Hamilton

## The mechanical city

By 1929, when Adrien Hébert — the son of the celebrated sculptor of church statues, Louis-Philippe Hébert — produced this curiously drab painting (shown at the left), he was already more fascinated by the machines than the people. The foreground is taken up by a car and an electric trolley; the liveliest part of the picture is the burst of smoke and steam erupting from the locomotive in the background. Later in life, Adrien took over his father's famous wood-carving studio. But, just as his talent for painting had never been more than ordinary, his gift for sculpture was limited. The studio went into decline and with it one of the great traditions of Canadian art — the wood carvers of Quebec.

Pegi Nicol MacLeod
*Gathering of People* / n.d.   water-colour   25 x 39
J. S. McLean Collection, Toronto

## The playful people

The crowded village square that caught Pegi Nicol MacLeod's eye was probably near Fredericton, N.B., where she taught a summer course in painting at the university every year. She lived the rest of the year in New York, where "she felt completely frustrated if she didn't complete at least a water colour or an oil sketch every day." Unlike most Canadian painters, she was interested more in people than things. She painted them wherever she found enough of them milling around to give her the sense of excitement she was forever trying to catch on canvas.

Goodridge Roberts / *Yellow Nude on Red Carpet* / 1961    oil on board    48 x 60 / James Borcoman, Ottawa

John Lyman
*Femmes sur la Plage*
c. 1950   oil on composition board   24 x 30
Hamilton Art Gallery

## Out of her time

John Lyman studied under Matisse in Paris before the first World War, and although he painted the nude at the left around 1950 she could easily have been on the beach at Cannes in 1907. More easily, perhaps, than on the beach in Lyman's native Montreal, for the suggestion that women sunbathe nude where children play and sailboats pass close by is a touch of fiction that Lyman has slipped straight-faced into his otherwise literal painting. Lyman is a critic as well as a painter. He is greatly respected for the encouragement he has given young painters in Montreal, where he was a professor of fine art at McGill University.

Edwin Holgate
*Nude in a Landscape*
n.d.   oil on canvas   29 x 46
National Gallery of Canada

## Out of her place

Edwin Holgate went on a painting expedition with A. Y. Jackson to the Skeena River in B.C. during 1926, and five years later he became a member of the Group of Seven. Holgate tried to combine the Group's favourite subject matter, the harsh northern landscape, with what increasingly became his own, the female figure. The result was cited by at least one critic as an unfortunate example of the influence of the National Style. Holgate is also known for his strong wood cuts and for murals in the Château Laurier and the Hotel Vancouver, but his finest achievements are his simple, almost monumental portraits, like one of Stephen Leacock that is now in the National Gallery.

Louis de Niverville
*The Family Group*
1961   oil on canvas   46 x 74¹/₂
Mr. and Mrs. Percy Waxer, Toronto

## The first signs of an overwhelming sadness

Louis de Niverville's career as a painter has been divided into two almost equal parts. In the first he became almost instantly famous for his wit, brightness and ability to pass on the pleasure he seemed to take in his drawings and paintings. For a young, new artist, his sales were phenomenal. Then, at the time he painted *The Family Group* (above), his pictures lost the joy they had transmitted so powerfully. "Around the picture," a critic wrote of *The Family Group*, "he wraps a cloak of serenity, composed equally of straight-faced humour and solemn, classical design." But some of the paintings in the same show were called sick, and sales fell off. In de Niverville's next show, in 1963, many of his people had become grotesque—and the sharper the horror they communicated, the slower the market for de Niverville's paintings, although to many critics they seemed far more penetrating and assured than his earlier, popular work. In 1964-65 de Niverville went to Europe and then Mexico. "The trip to Mexico," he said later, "had almost more influence on me than the eight months in Europe. My paintings once again are lush, full of the sea and nature. Out of this my work has become more artificial, more full of fantasy than ever."

De Niverville describes his paintings as "a combination of symbols and feelings." After looking at a picture like *The Family Group* for a while, it seems likely that he is telling the story of his life over and over again, every time adding something from a different dream.

Tom Hodgson
*Two Faces of Sophia*
1962   oil and collage on canvas   82 x 62
Courtesy of the Artist

## The qualities
## of a sex goddess

Tom Hodgson believes all women are beautiful, and Sophia Loren is *more* beautiful. Therefore he painted Miss Loren, and it is this painting that appears (left) here. Just where, one may ask, is the likeness? According to one critic, the painting captures the movie star's "essential vitality of spirit; her romantic quality in the role of sex goddess; and the fragmented personality left behind after the collision between the star, who is public property, and the woman, who is not." Hodgson is a superlative craftsman with colour, and his best paintings have a swashbuckling vitality. This is no more than poetic justice. Hodgson was twice, in 1952 and 1956, an Olympic paddler for Canada. He has been a highly successful advertising agency art director, and is now a free-lance commercial artist.

Robert Hedrick / *Homage to Goya* / 1964   oil on canvas   60 x 84
Courtesy Jerrold Morris International Gallery, Toronto

## The quality of Goya

Critics have called Robert Hedrick an "action painter," to which Hedrick has replied, "I detest labels for art. They're a kind of amateur hipsterism." Art might be easier for non-artists to enjoy if all critics and painters felt the same way about labels. Hedrick has studied in both Mexico and Spain, and it was the last trip, of course, that was responsible for *Homage to Goya* (left). "I tend to restrict my means," Hedrick says, "producing a very tight thing –almost classical."

Graham Coughtry
*Two Figures* / 1964   oil on canvas   72 x 60
Courtesy The Isaacs Gallery, Toronto

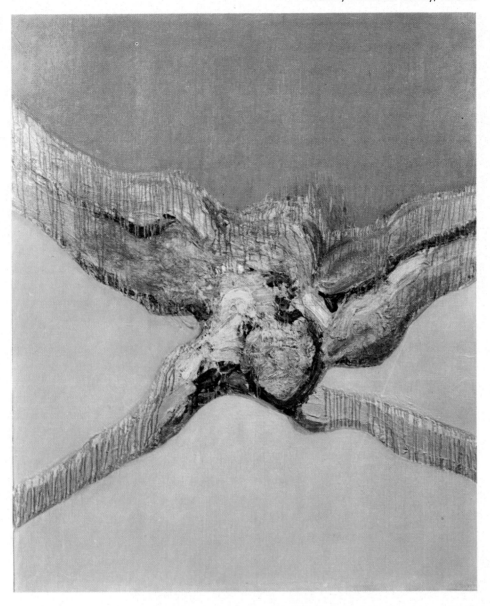

## An emotional regard for the figure

In 1961, when the attention of painters in Toronto and elsewhere was beginning to turn away from Abstract Expressionism, Graham Coughtry had a one-man show of figure paintings. They made him, almost overnight, one of the most celebrated painters in Canada. He now has a waiting list for new paintings, at two thousand dollars for a five-foot by six-foot canvas, which is an almost unheard-of figure for Canadian buyers to pay a young Canadian artist. Since 1963 Coughtry has painted a series of two-figure studies, of which the picture above is one.

"The initial impulse," he has observed, "is a regard for the figure itself. Then a way of painting emerges, and this is the most important outcome."

Michael Snow
*Seated Nude* / 1955   painted collage   40 x 30
Mr. and Mrs. Percy Waxer, Toronto

## A link between jazz and the modern woman

At one time, Michael Snow earned his living playing the piano in a Toronto jazz band. In both jazz and painting, he said at the time, "one starts with a theme and through improvisation and organization one places his personal stamp on the work ... Actually, all I want to do is present some kind of moving image using all the elements of painting: colour, line, form, texture." As one way to get the motion he is after, Snow has done a lot of work on animated films (his wife, Joyce Wieland – page 113 – once organized a film company; they called it Groovy Films, Inc.). Looking, again, for a sense of motion, he worked out the vaguely multiple-exposure technique that gives the *Seated Nude* reproduced here (left) the look of a woman who can't sit still. At first glance her body seems to be a grotesque exaggeration of the female figure, but after a longer look it can be seen to combine strong sensuality with a delicate, flowing line. Snow has worked in a great variety of styles and forms, but he retains by instinct a lyrical quality in everything he does.

Jean Dallaire
*Composition: Femme Assise*
1955   oil on canvas
42³/₄ x 59¹/₂
National Gallery of Canada

John Fox
*Mirror Reflections*
1963   oil on canvas   32 x 32
Courtesy Continental Galleries, Montreal

## Seeing both sides of the same person

The unaided eye can't do it, so painters of every generation have worked out their own devices for showing one figure from front and back in the same painting. Picasso went nature one better and combined both views in the same figure. John Fox, a shy, reserved painter who was born in Montreal in 1933, used the conventional device of a full-length mirror (right). Fox paints in the Post-Impressionist style; his subject, very often, is the streets of the city.

## Gay but threatened

When France fell in World War II Jean Dallaire was in Paris studying art. He was a prisoner of war from 1940 until 1945. After the war he studied tapestry-making in France, then came back to his native Quebec to teach at l'Ecole des Beaux Arts in Montreal. Tapestry was in small demand, and he joined the National Film Board, where he specialized in historical films. He died in November 1965.

In all of Dallaire's work there is the same calculated distortion that makes his sharp-nosed *Femme Assise* (right) both slightly ludicrous and slightly ominous. This may well be a legacy of five years in the prison camps, where escape into sardonic fantasies was therapeutic. Whatever the reason, Dallaire is one of the few Canadian painters who has stayed with the original form of Surrealism most of his life. His dreams have never been the nightmares that many Surrealists painted, nor have they been entirely gay. They include a threat.

89

# The nature of human sympathy and response

Bruno Bobak's tryptych (below) of variations on human affection is a logical outcome of his chief concern in recent years. He wants to bring humanity back into painting; to deal with every subject in terms of human sympathy and response.

Bobak became painter-in-resi- dence at the University of New Brunswick in 1960, after an unusu- ally crowded career. He had been a war artist overseas in his early twenties, a teacher in his adopted Vancouver, a government artist in Ottawa, and a student in London on a Canadian government over- seas fellowship. He was first a me- ticulous water-colourist, recording with devotion the fine details of nature on the West Coast. More lately he has painted large Expres- sionist oils, often dealing with the Canadian landscape but always showing the presence of man.

Bruno Bobak / *The Seasons* / 1963-4   oil on canvas   40 x 30 outer panels / 48 x 40 centre panel / Courtesy of the Artist

# The pleasures of the mind and the flesh

When Alfred Pellan returned from France to Canada in 1940, a Mont- real critic wrote: "He brings an almost unforgivable exuberance and sense of health into our other- wise anaemic artistic circles." He moved into an old stone farmhouse north of Montreal, where he still lives. He works, with enormous energy, in a studio he built himself; he is a man of unusual strength, with hands that look as though they could twist horseshoes. He has always been fascinated by the infinite number of ways a line can be forced to carry out its own logic (he once spent an entire afternoon telling an interviewer how much he admired the American cartoonist Steinberg). Some of that fascina- tion is apparent in *Sur la Plage* (opposite page). Unlike most "major" painters, Pellan has never burdened his paintings with cruel or tragic overtones. The expression of the foreground profile in this painting is benign, and the people on the beach are having a ball. In many of his paintings the people are clearly clowning.

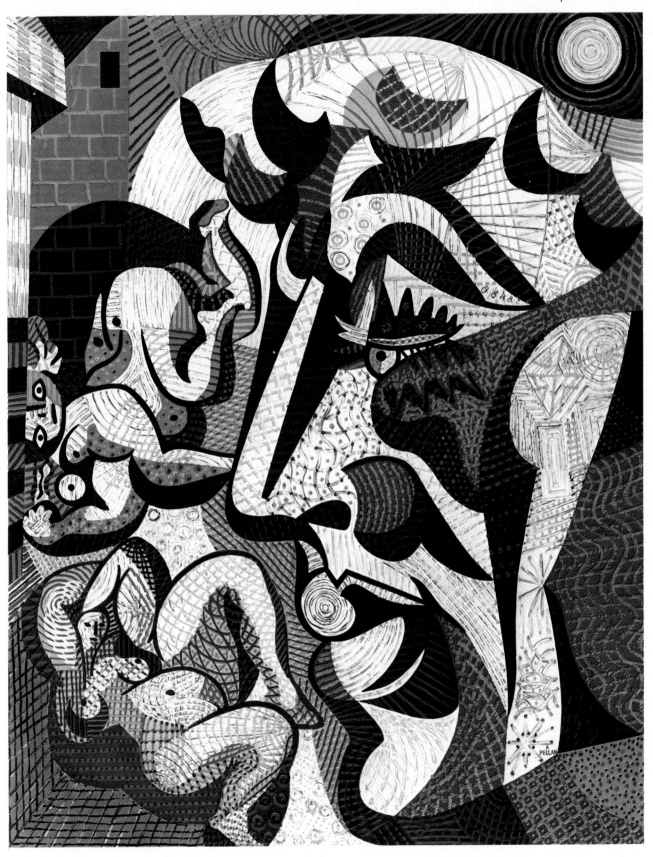

Alfred Pellan
*Sur La Plage* / 1952   oil   81³/₄ x 66
National Gallery of Canada

Dennis Burton
*Mother, Earth, Love* / 1965　oil on canvas　60 x 80
Art Gallery of Toronto

# A closer look
## at what's underneath,
## in colour

"Garterbeltmania" is the name Dennis Burton gives the series of underwear pictures he started in 1964. *Mother, Earth, Love* (above) is one of the most elaborate of the series. A psychoanalyst would probably take one look at it and describe Burton as a fetishist. Burton has his own explanation: "These garments provide a beautiful set of movable, distortable shapes and forms with which to deal as a painter. The Twentieth Century Woman is a packaged commodity. She is present . . . only as a sex symbol. I don't quarrel with this use of woman as the most deliciously containerized commodity available. But I do quarrel with the resulting loss of her humanity. In my work, I express my love for the container, and especially for its contents." Burton grew up in Lethbridge, where, he says, he was living in a cultural desert. As a boy he had only one contact with art; magazines. They were supplemented once a year by the Eaton's and Simpson's catalogues. This last fact may do more to account for his later love of pictorialized underwear than all his own explanations.

# Feelings & Ideas

The twentieth century arrived late for Canadian painters. By 1900 Freud and modern physics had opened up new ways of looking inward at the levels of the mind below conscious thought, and outward at a world made up of dancing particles of energy whose common denominator was light. Art was never the same again. European painters began rearranging the natural world according to their own ideas, or painting their inner feelings without any reference to the real things that caused them. A certain amount of confusion arose when critics started calling this kind of painting "abstract" art. All art is abstract; the word simply means to draw from, and a prehistoric cave-painter or Picasso were both drawing from themselves and the world around them whatever they needed to make their pictures. But an alternate meaning of abstract is "not easy to understand," and this has become an uncomfortably accurate description of many paintings the word is used to describe. Some of these paintings are hard to understand because they are just stunts with paint, empty of any quality worth understanding. Others are deliberately recondite or ambiguous, like the twentieth-century world they were painted in.

For a long time, the problem of understanding them, or even tolerating them, defeated not only the Canadian public but Canadian painters as well. When World War II drove Alfred Pellan home to Quebec from Paris, he got a teaching job at Montreal's Ecole des Beaux Arts. Just three years before the war he had been turned down for the same job because he spoke well of the ideas brought to painting by the men he had admired in Europe — Picasso, Ernst, Bracque and Miro. In 1945, when the school's administrators refused to hang experimental paintings by two of his students, the young painters ran through the nearby streets chanting "Vive Pellan! A bas Maillard!" Although the academic establishment then dominated Canadian art, Charles Maillard, the principal of the Ecole des Beaux Arts, had to go; Pellan, the unorthodox teacher, was asked to stay. That was the day Canadian painting entered the twentieth century, and before long, spurred on by Pellan and a much different kind of painter, Paul-Emile Borduas, there was a vigorous, noisy, excited new school of painting in Montreal.

The excitement made little impression, at first, in Toronto or elsewhere in English-speaking Canada. When a loose group of young Toronto artists who called themselves Painters Eleven began to test some of the same ideas in the early 1950s, the art establishment met them with such stony indifference that they hustled department stores and restaurants for space to display their paintings. None of them was admitted to the Ontario Society of Artists until 1953.

Like the Montreal painters a few years earlier, the Painters Eleven group formed around two men, although neither was a dominant figure on the near-heroic scale of Borduas and Pellan. Jock Macdonald was already in his fifties, a superb teacher but a painter who had not yet mastered the new ideas he had been working with in isolation for close to twenty years. Oscar Cahén was a post-war immigrant who had studied in most of the art capitals of Europe. He set a new standard of sophistication for magazine illustration in Canada; Cahén lived up to his income, and his dashing style of life probably impressed the young painters around him as much as his ideas about art did.

One of the first patterns that strikes the eye among the paintings on the following pages is the early turn toward these new ways of painting on the west coast. In 1940, when Lawren Harris chose to live in Vancouver, he was already beginning to paint his austere symbols of the arctic; B. C. Binning and Jack Shadbolt were respected (and gainfully employed) members of the Vancouver art establishment before Painters Eleven began to earn the scorn of Toronto, let alone its later esteem.

By 1965, indeed, there were some critics who claimed that the most adventurous painting in Canada was being done by the new Saskatchewan school led by Ronald Bloore and Kenneth Lochhead. Canadian painting, which had long — perhaps too long — had a National Style, seemed at last to have a national horizon.

Lionel LeMoine FitzGerald
*Three Apples on a Plate*
1949   water-colour with chalk dots   10³/₄ x 15
Douglas Duncan, Toronto

# How to paint an apple by starting inside and trying to push it out

From the 1920s to the 1940s, when most Canadian painters were using rocks and trees for subjects and patriotism for inspiration, LeMoine FitzGerald was looking for new ways to see the simplest things in the world. Things like a jug, a book, or an apple: he painted apples over and over again, trying, he said, "to get inside the object and push it out rather than merely building it up from the outer aspect." This is the kind of remark that often makes painters sound a little like confidence men–it doesn't seem to mean anything. But in this case, a close

look at the apples in the painting above helps make sense of what FitzGerald was saying. Although he painted with a light, soft touch in the plainest colours he could find, his apples are more than hollow skins. Their full weight is on the plate.

FitzGerald was not only a thoughtful painter; he wanted his paintings to lead other people back to the habit of reflection. Since so much of what interested him was going on in his own mind, he saw almost no reason to stir out of his native Winnipeg. Once, when he

thought the impressionist style of his early painting was getting too easy for him, he went to New York for a winter and studied at the Art Students' League. And once he stayed with his son in Mexico for two years. But during the rest of his life he stayed in and around Winnipeg, teaching and painting. Towards the end he was a recluse, too busy with paint to make time for people. "I get so damn mad," he once wrote, "when I get started on a train of thought . . . then this business of food and shelter" interrupts it.

## What "magic" means:
## too real to be true

When the European Surrealists painted a dream a few generations ago, they made up an entire hallucination—a weird situation and the characters to go with it. Now, when the "magic realists" paint a dream, they make up nothing. Every detail is a precise copy of the real thing. But the action is frozen, like one frame cut out of a moving picture, and the angle is usually extreme and unexpected.

Seen this way, ordinary things like a horse or a train are suddenly too real to be true; they have become the timeless symbols for real things that are only met in dreams or magic. Alex Colville, of Sackville, N.B., is one of the leaders of this school of painting. The style has become so popular in the U.S. that relatively few examples are seen in Canada. When Colville finishes a painting (he turns out only three or four a year) he sends a photograph to one of the American collectors on his waiting list, and looks for a cheque by return mail. This is unusual enough; what makes it striking is that the price is rarely less than eight thousand dollars. (The only painting he offered at the 1965 Montreal Spring Show went for nine thousand.) Young Canadian painters who have adopted the same style, some of them Colville's students, usually leave early in their careers for New York. There, even as unknowns, they can ask as much as four hundred dollars for a small painting.

The rush to buy Colville's paintings has made one-man shows of his work rare. But he has represented Canada at large international exhibitions such as the 1964 show of Canadian painting at the Tate Gallery in London. He is probably one of the two or three best-known living Canadian painters—outside Canada.

Bertram Charles Binning / *Ghost Ships*
1949   oil on paper board   36 x 17 / Art Gallery of Toronto

## From the happy coast

B. C. Binning is an art patriot of a different colour. For one thing, he limits his real enthusiasm to B.C., where he has lived since he was a student of Frederick Varley in the 1930s. For another, he challenges the north woods school of nationalist painting. He wants to show people that "Canadian art need not be only grim, rugged and forbidding"; in fact, he said in 1946, "I am convinced that there is something happy about this coast." He has been trying to paint the happy coast ever since, most often by making almost abstract geometric patterns out of ships and shorelines. His mural in the lobby of Vancouver's B.C. Power Building looks like part of the original design. This is natural; Binning was first an architect.

## From the eerie north

Jack Shadbolt's far different view of the west coast is summed up by the painting at the right, in which, he says, he is trying to paint the "mystery and dimension of the northern horizon." Shadbolt began, like Emily Carr, with great admiration for west coast Indian art. During World War II he turned to more abstract images as a way to convey the horror of what he saw as a war artist. Since the war, he has become the best known of the painters who have worked on the west coast. His paintings have appeared in the best of the international exhibitions—the Venice Biennale of 1956; the Guggenheim International of 1958—and he has become an important source of ideas for younger west coast painters. At the Vancouver School of Art, he is head of the drawing and painting section.

J. L. Shadbolt
*Northern Emblem #7*
1964   oil and lucite on canvas   50 x 40
Courtesy of the Artist

Alfred Pellan
*Nature Morte au Verre de Cristal* / 1942-3    oil on canvas    25¹/₂ x 24
Camille Hébert, Montreal

## Why flat apples?

According to Alfred Pellan, the revolutionary leader of post-war painting in Montreal (see page 91), "a painter should be like a fisherman. He keeps the fish he wants, and throws the rest back." In the still-life on the opposite page, Pellan has kept the horizon, the table-top, and the shape of apples. But he has thrown back perspective. The apples are flat Cubist shapes, and the *décor* he has added is all on one plane.

## What *very* modern art is all about: paint

Although Jean-Paul Riopelle was born in Montreal and was already an accomplished painter when he moved to Paris in 1948, he is regarded as French by everyone but Canadians. "He has exemplified, more perfectly than any other painter in the world, the dominant tendencies of post-1948 art," a critic said in the early 1960s. "In his work, the artist's thoughts are submerged in favour of the act of painting itself." This kind of art (Abstract Expressionism here, Tachism in France) can't be taken in at a glance. The horse and trough in the painting above are there, if you look long and hard, but it's the paint that counts. Riopelle resembles Chico Marx, and even lives a little like a movie star—he collects Bugatti cars and owns a yacht. How? A small Riopelle sells for one thousand dollars, a large one for thirty thousand, and they sell as fast as he paints.

Paul-Emile Borduas
*L'Etoile Noir* / 1957   oil on canvas   63³/₄ x 51¹/₄
Montreal Museum of Fine Arts

## Epitaph for a rebel

If Pellan (page 100) was the leader of Quebec's post-war revolt in art, Paul-Emile Borduas was its prophet. His end, like most prophets', was tragic. "He fought with his colleagues, he split the Contemporary Art Society which he had helped found, he turned against the younger artists who were his apostles, left his wife and family, his friends and country, and died virtually alone in self-imposed exile." He also created true beauty. *L'Etoile Noire,* the painting on the opposite page, was awarded posthumously the Guggenheim National Section Award in 1960 as the best Canadian painting of that year.

## Tribute to a woman

Quebec may have more first-rank active woman painters than any other art centre in the world. Micheline Beauchemin, Shirley Wales, Tobie Steinhouse, Ghitta Caiserman are all well-known painters, and Marcelle Ferron and Rita Letendre are among the best-known Quebec-born artists. Miss Letendre (right, above) paints in the Tachist style of Borduas, but her results are passionate rather than cool.

## Praise for a poet

Until Jean McEwen (right) was in his early twenties he thought of himself as a poet, and his verse was published in such Quebec quarterlies as *La Nouvelle Relève*. He turned to painting when he decided his verse wasn't good enough, in 1947, but most critics have claimed to see poetic qualities in all his painting since. He often paints with his fingers, and tries to harmonize colour and light.

Jean McEwen / *Le Drapeau inconnu* / 1964   oil on canvas   80 x 75
Galerie Agnes Lefort, Montreal

Oscar Cahén
*Trophy* / 1955-6   oil on masonite   49³/₄ x 32
Art Gallery of Toronto

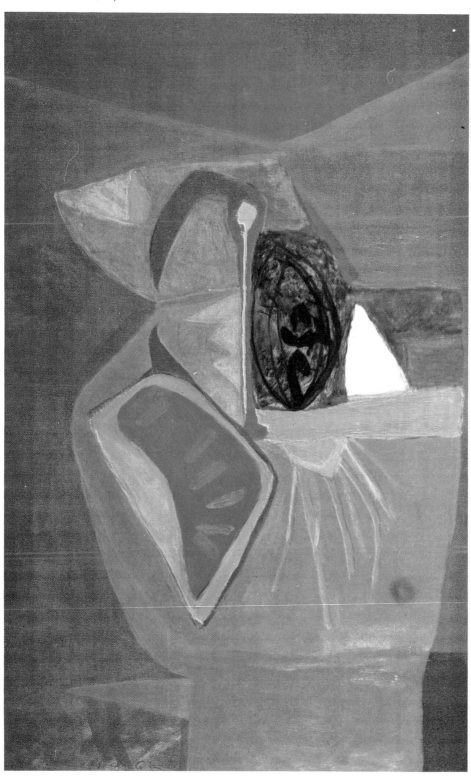

## Pushing and pulling

By the time Oscar Cahén killed himself driving a fast car in 1956 he had already studied painting in his native Copenhagen, in Berlin, Prague, Paris and London; had become the leading magazine illustrator in Canada; and had helped change the stance of fine art in Toronto from backward-looking formalism to forward-looking experimentation. Yet he was only forty when he died.

Just before his death, an interviewer asked him to explain his paintings. "Why don't you go out and ask a bird what his song means?" Cahén said. "I'm not interested in telling a story . . . When I paint, I set down the pushing and pulling of my emotions." The emotion that critics have found in *Trophy* (left) is fear: "the forms are strangely menacing."

## Why the paint is thin

Jack Bush (opposite page) is a Post-Painterly Abstractionist, of all labels for schools of painting the one hardest for most people to understand (or, for that matter, to take seriously). Bush says he is interested in "the power below the surface" of his canvas. The style calls for thin paint, to avoid depth and reflected light; loose brush strokes for anonymity from painter to painter; and images "aimed at eloquence." Some viewers see little eloquence or feeling in these paintings, but one leading American critic calls Bush Canada's most important painter.

Jack Bush
*Paris No. Two* / 1962-3   acrylic on canvas   96 x 72
Mr. and Mrs. John C. Parkin, Toronto

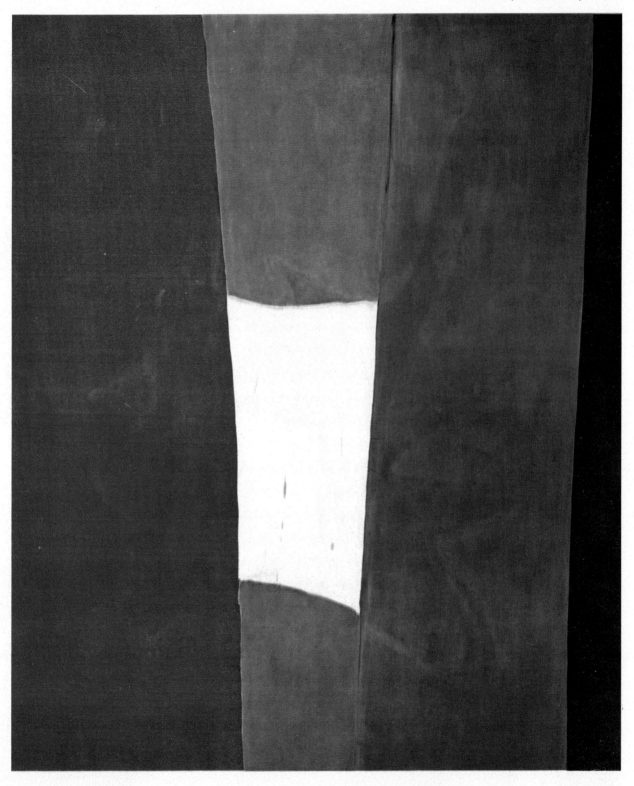

Jock Macdonald
*Fleeting Breath* / 1959   oil on canvas   48 x 58⅝
Art Gallery of Toronto

## Joyful paintings that almost came too late

Despite a towering reputation as a teacher, J.W.G. (or Jock, as he began calling himself in 1954) Macdonald was regarded as a second-rank painter until his sixtieth year, in 1957. Then, as one critic said, "he produced a series of canvases that marked him unmistakably as one of our creative leaders . . . He had emerged with abstracts of exceptional richness and vitality." Two of those abstracts appear here. *Fleeting Breath* (left) is one of the most beautiful and accomplished of all Macdonald's paintings. He had been experimenting with the successive styles of "modern" art ever since he reached Vancouver from Scotland in 1926, and although his paintings had been original they had appeared tight, and even forced, to most critics. Then he visited Hans Hofmann, the great German teacher who was responsible for the rise of Abstract Expressionism in the United States during the 1950s, and seemed to find the style he had been looking for. Between *Fleeting Breath* and *All Things Prevail* (above), the last painting he finished before his death in 1960, his style was loose and free, his paint vivid, and his sharp pleasure in his work always there to see in the finished canvas. He was experimenting with colour: a series of paintings emphasizing red, then a series stressing brown; then white; and finally the brilliant sunlit colours at the top of this page. But although he was working well, he was working too much, teaching full-time at the Ontario College of Art and painting far into the night. He wanted money to buy more time for painting. But there was no more time; he died in December, probably of overwork.

Jack Reppen
*Valley of the Aztecs* / 1962    oil / mixed media on board    48 x 48
Mr. and Mrs. Walter Moos, Toronto

## Ending at the start

Most of the people who had watched Jack Reppen develop as a painter thought he was just beginning to reach artistic maturity when he died of cancer in 1964, at twenty-nine. He had been an incredibly active young man: art director for a life insurance company; sports page cartoonist for a newspaper; amateur house designer; student of jazz; muralist and painter. This painting (left) is one of a series in which he tried to recreate ancient ruins he had seen in Mexico. "It was his idea," a critic said, "that a painting . . . could sum up the stream of history."

William Ronald / *Gypsy* / 1959    oil on canvas    60 x 70
Dr. and Mrs. S. L. Wax, Toronto

## The price of escape

When William Ronald painted *Gypsy* (left) in 1959 he was moving away from Abstract Expressionism, which had been his style for several years, toward a more symbolic kind of abstraction. The swirl of harsh colour in *Gypsy* just might be the kind of unthought Expressionist pattern that is painted first and named second — but the orderly bars closing in from all sides have obviously been planned in advance. In 1955 Ronald left Toronto for New York, where he is now regarded as an American painter. He has what he calls a "love-hate relationship" with Canada, largely because Toronto art circles were hostile to the new style he was trying to work out in the early 1950s. Now his New York prices — three to four thousand dollars for a medium-sized canvas — make it hard for him to sell in Canada.

# Doing everything well

In 1953 Harold Town bought a second-hand lithograph press from Duncan Macpherson (who later, of course, became one of the world's great political cartoonists). The first prints he made sold – slowly – for fifteen dollars each. "I worked exclusively in black and red," Town said later, "for the deep symbolic reason that those were the colours that had come with the press." Between 1953 and 1956 Town went on to develop a new technique that has made him one of the most honoured print-makers in the world. He combines methods borrowed from lithography, linocut, etching and aquatint with the application of stencils, overprinting and print-on-print printing. From each set of plates he makes only one print, and he has coined a name for the results: he calls them Single Autographic Prints. *Gateway to Atlantis* (right, above) is one of them.

But Town is a protean artist, and in trying everything he has also produced many of the most accomplished collages ever turned out in Canada. Several critics have said that *Monument to Currelly* (right) is the best of these. Currelly was director of the Royal Ontario Museum during Town's youth in Toronto. "The museum has played an immense role in my creative life," Town has said. "To me it's like a miracle, like one of those Chinese boxes that open up, full of miracles. Currelly created a toy for the whole city." Echoes of the sights Town saw in Currelly's museum have appeared in his art ever since: Babylonian, Assyrian, Chinese, and west coast Indian. His collages are like a museum of his life.

John Meredith
*Bengal 1* / 1962   oil on canvas   42 x 52
Courtesy Isaacs Gallery, Toronto

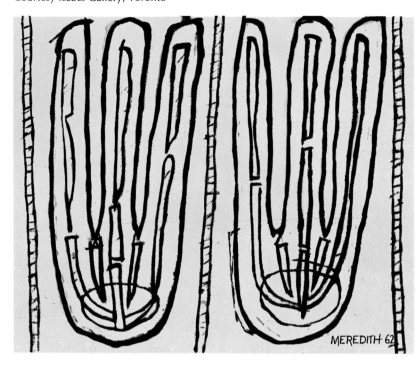

## Like nothing else

A painter like John Meredith is a rarity: until he was thirty he lived alone in a studio in his parents' home in Fergus, Ont., and although he has since moved to Toronto he still lives and works in isolation, taking advice or adopting ideas from nobody. According to his brother, the painter William Ronald (page 108), Meredith's paintings are thus unique, "because there's nothing to compare them with." Like *Bengal I* (left) his paintings are often built on a pattern of vertical stripes that, in one critic's words, "bend, weave, merge, then pull apart again . . . exotic, jingly, oddly convincing."

Gordon Rayner
*Magnetewan #2* / 1965   co-polymer acrylic on canvas   60 x 60
Courtesy Isaacs Gallery, Toronto

## Always something new

His dealer says of Gordon Rayner: "Many artists claim each new painting is a totally new experience. I believe Rayner comes closest to exemplifying this . . . in each show he has had four or five gems, and four or five works that ought to have been burned." Rayner is as tall as a sandwich man on stilts and affects a huge moustache, long hair, and the personal style of a jazz musician (he and three other Toronto painters formed The Artists' Jazz Band in 1962). Not long after that he discovered acrylic paint; a malleable plastic harmless to cheap cotton canvas that oils would destroy. Acrylics can duplicate both the transparency of water colours and the depth of oils. *Magnetewan II* (left) is one of the consistently fine landscapes Rayner has painted with plastic paint.

Kenneth Lochhead
*Dark Green Centre*
1963   acrylic on canvas   81³/₄ x 80
Art Gallery of Toronto

## A universal image for life on the prairies – perhaps

In 1953 Kenneth Lochhead, who had been director of the school of art at the University of Saskatchewan for three years, said he was "getting to know more of the life of the prairie, and trying to apply (to it) a universal image." Ten years later he was painting pictures like the one above, in the style called Post-Painterly Abstraction. "He has broken through to pure flat colour stated in shapes that approach 'geometry' without really touching it ... It remains to be seen whether (he) will pursue his new vision of colour with the required tenacity, and above all, nerve." The critic didn't say whether a painting like this has anything to do with life on the prairie.

Well, does it?

Gerald Gladstone
*Periphery Painting #7* / 1963   oil on canvas   54 x 43
Mr. and Mrs. William Kilbourn, Toronto

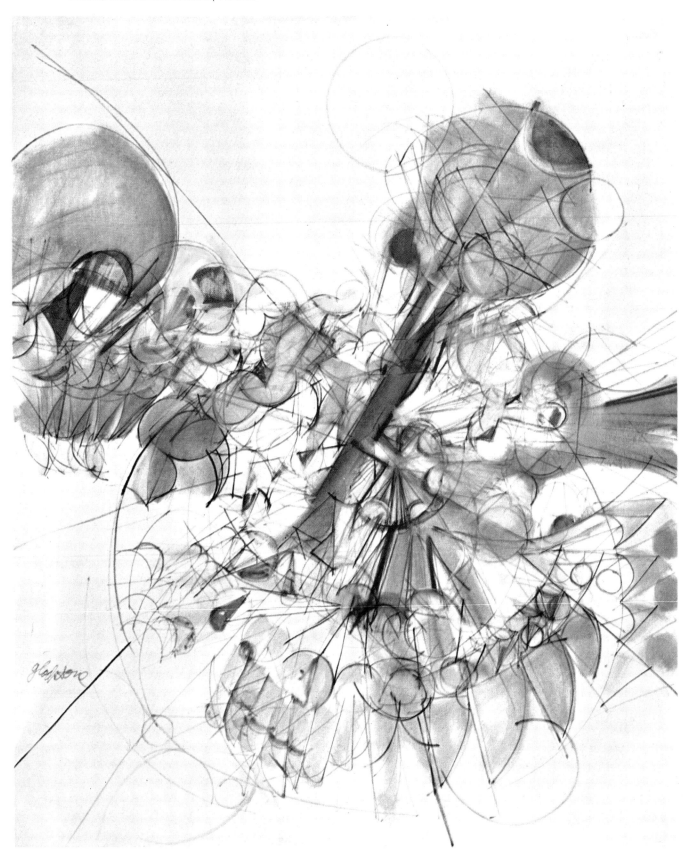

Ronald Bloore
*Byzantium*
1961   oil on masonite   48 x 48
Mr. and Mrs. Michael Taylor, Toronto

## Self-advertisements

Gerald Gladstone says his sculptures are works of genius, and many critics agree with him. He has said little about his paintings, but they are mainly two-dimensional versions of the same shapes. At the time he did the *Periphery Painting* (opposite page) he used only blue, yellow and red when he painted, and used a compass dipped in paint for the main curves. But the painting leaps at the eye like an explosion; it has a highly original, violent beauty. Gladstone also plays the flute (superbly, by his own admission) and writes mathematical philosophy. Like this: "We are in the thin end of a cone-shaped universe and are moving toward the fat end."

## Instant admiration

Between 1961 and 1963 Ronald Bloore went from complete anonymity outside a small circle of artists in Saskatchewan to popular and critical recognition as one of the major figures in Canadian painting. Most of his paintings are simple abstract designs set on a white background. *Byzantium* (above, right) is more elaborate than his work usually is, but just as elegant.

## Love and satire

The objects hung out to dry in the upper right-hand corner of Joyce Wieland's *Cooling Room* are hearts, like the ones on left-over valentines. Love is what Miss Wieland (who is married to the painter Michael Snow, pp. 76 and 88) usually comments on in her art, and very often her comment is a wry, occasionally a sad or vulgar, one.

Joyce Wieland / *Cooling Room II*
1964   painted construction on board   37 x 29 x 5
Courtesy Isaacs Gallery, Toronto

## Twenty works in one

Although it has the deep colour and rich texture of a painting, this is something
else – the fifth of twenty almost identical prints made on laminated paper by a
hand press. The artist, a thin, high-strung Québecois named Yves Gaucher, is
one of the leading reasons why Canadian print-makers now have a high reputation
around the world. He has been experimenting with prints ever since he was
expelled in the early 1950s from a Montreal *collège classique* for drawing
"questionable pictures." Since then he has won a fistful of international awards,
among them the Second Grand Award of the Triennial Exhibition of Prints at
Grenchen, Switzerland, in 1964.

## More than op art

Optical (or op) art, the craze that followed pop art in the early 1960s, happened when painters began playing with the eye-teasing designs that have intrigued school children for centuries – the kind that change their form when you look at them hard enough. Claude Tousignant, a reserved man who shelters behind an aggressive moustache, is the most interesting of the Canadian painters who have experimented with this device. But unlike the painters who have gone straight for the geometric trick – the closed box that becomes an open box as you stare at it, and all the standard variations – he has built into the trap for the eye his earlier liking for rich colours and emotional effects. Most of his op paintings are based on a bulls-eye design, like this one. Standing in front of it, a viewer is meant to feel that the painting is beginning to swirl away from the wall and surround him. The intention works.

Guido Molinari
*Multinoir* / n.d.   oil on canvas   45 x 49
Art Gallery of Toronto

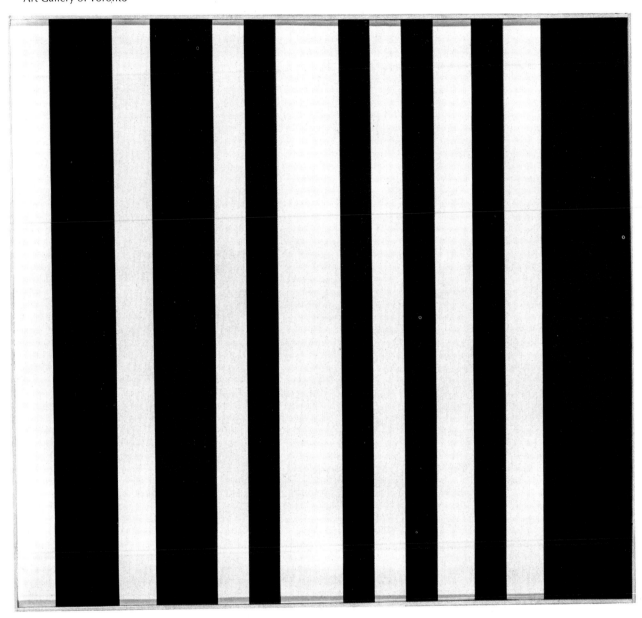

## Saying the things that words can't say

There is nothing in his paintings, Guido Molinari insists, that can be passed on verbally. This may be partly because Molinari paints nothing but stripes — none narrower than one inch, none wider than fifteen inches — and when you have said that, what else is there? He *does* say this: "My colour has absolute autonomy as the carrier of emotional content . . . My present goal is absolute equilibrium." Molinari is professor of design at the Ecole des Beaux Arts in Montreal, and perhaps the most influential of the French-Canadian painters in his own generation (he was born in Montreal in 1933).

# The Loners

SEARCHING FOR BEAUTY IN PAIN AND SOLITUDE.

The towering geniuses of art find new ways of seeing the world. These are the Leonardos, the Rembrandts, the Cézannes; in Canada's first hundred years there has been no native painter like this. The good practising painters work within the kinds of vision created by the towering geniuses, refining and developing their ideas; most of the painters in this book are good practising painters. Then there is a third group, very small and far more difficult to categorize. These are the loners, the great solitary figures who master their own ways of painting their own worlds but never quite succeed in imposing their ideas on a generation or a century. Of these, Canada has had at least three: Emily Carr, David Milne and Ozias Leduc. They were all intensely, even painfully private people. Leduc lived almost all his life in partial or, at some seasons, complete seclusion in an habitant village called St. Hilaire. Milne moved restlessly from village to village in his native Ontario and in upstate New York, carrying on most of his traffic with the larger world by writing letters, chronically and skilfully. Emily Carr spent part of her life plagued by mosquitoes and sheltering in graves at inaccessible Indian villages on the west coast, and during most of those years she was as unknown in the rest of Canada as any of the Indians she painted. All three were recognized as major figures in Canada's artistic history only when they were very close to, or at, the ends of their lives. Leduc's national reputation began with the retrospective show of his work assembled by the National Gallery after his death in 1955. (By then his pupil, Paul-Emile Borduas, who by a lucky chance had been born in Leduc's village, was already a celebrity of Quebec's avant garde, if not a popular favourite.) Milne was still dependent on the loyal support of a few patrons when he died in 1953. Emily Carr was fifty-seven when the National Gallery discovered her, but she confessed she knew nothing of the National Gallery. All three painted superb pictures, stamped with the strong, sure sense of their own visual idiom that sets them apart at first sight from the work of any other painter in the world. This is one of the marks of genius. It is apparent in the paintings on the next six pages.

Neige Dorée / 1916   oil on canvas   54 x 30
National Gallery of Canada

# Ozias Leduc

## The link with history

The lifetime of Ozias Leduc came close to the lifetime of confederated Canada — he was born in 1864, and died in 1955. For most of that time he was almost unknown outside a small circle of art experts in Quebec. When some of his paintings finally began circulating among Canadian galleries elsewhere, they were hailed as brilliant discoveries. But in 1954 a leading Montreal critic had written: "Leduc is the unique tangible link that we have with the first century of art history in Canada. Without him, there would be no continuity." Leduc's singular gift was to paint well, sometimes superbly, in many of the new styles of painting that developed during his extraordinary lifetime. He began as a church decorator in the 1880s. In 1892 he won first prize for the best painting by an artist under thirty at the Spring Show of the Montreal Art Association. The painting was *Phrenologie* (far right), a brilliant example of the *trompe l'oeil* style that was then sweeping the United States. From experiments like this he usually moved back to religious themes, then forward again to fresh experiments: still-lifes, portraits, landscapes. He painted *Neige Dorée,* at the right, in 1916. While this remarkable painting belongs to no school, it is probably the first Canadian picture that uses some of the ideas of *art nouveau,* the European vogue that later helped shape the development of the Group of Seven and their National Style.

*Still Life: Phrenology* / 1892   oil on wood panel   13¹/₄ x 10³/₄
M  and Mme Maurice Corbeil, Montreal

*Blunden Harbour* / c. 1928-30   oil on canvas   51 x 37
National Gallery of Canada

# Emily Carr

## Painting a land like no other

The west coast and its rain forest are so rich in their colours and shapes that to a painter trained anywhere else on the continent they seem unpaintable. So Emily Carr was assured by an artist older and more celebrated than she. Common sense argued against trying; Miss Carr gave the rest of her life to the attempt, an adventure of pure gallantry. She faced down the opposition of her family and friends; the hostility of her neighbours; the demoralizing effects of poverty and the debilitating effects of physical exposure. Searching for the painter's skills she needed, she left home at eighteen to study in San Francisco, then in London; twenty years later she was studying again, this time in Paris. (Two of her paintings hung in the Salon d'Automne of 1911, the most controversial show in a year when the painters of Paris were breaking all the conventions of art.) She was finding the muscular new language she had needed to translate the rain forest into paint, but back home on the west coast her paintings attracted sneers and she herself scorn. During the next fifteen years the only people who talked her language were the Coast Indians. She understood their art, and painted a monumental record of it. They understood hers, and indeed it was paintings the anthropologist Marius Barbeau saw in their houses that finally made her awesome achievement known to the art establishment of the east. She was a great painter; perhaps the greatest of all woman painters.

*Scorned as Timber, Beloved of the Sky* / n.d.   oil on canvas   44 x 27
Vancouver Art Gallery

*Glass Jar and Blue Iris /* 1946    water-colour    14¼ x 21
Douglas Duncan, Toronto

# David Milne

## The thing that makes dynamite

"Feeling is the power that drives art," David Milne wrote five years before his death in 1953. Earlier, he had said, "The thing that makes a picture is the thing that makes dynamite – compression." (Milne was one of those painters who write well enough to depress writers.) "It isn't a fire in the grass; it is an explosion. Everything must hit at once." He meant it. All his life he moved from village to village in upstate New York and Ontario, from rundown houses to tarpaper shacks, not because he was particularly fond of rural seclusion but because he was too poor to live in the city. He took money from a series of friends and patrons like Vincent Massey and Douglas Duncan, but refused to give up any of his painting time to a paid job as a teacher. Finally he refused to stay married, on the grounds that to support his wife he would have to do more than paint. (He left her a curt note suggesting she get a divorce, and disappeared.) At a 1924 exhibition of his paintings in Montreal there was not a single sale. By the time of his death he was one of Canada's most honoured painters, although still one of the least prosperous. The location of his Toronto grave is lost; the headstone was a cheap one.

# A glossary of painting terms

| | |
|---|---|
| *Abstract Expressionism* | describes the painting done by a school of New York artists between 1945 and 1960. The best-known is Jackson Pollock, who had his first show in this style in 1943. The physical act of painting and expression of subconscious ideas or experiences dominate the method. Hans Hoffman was the great teacher during this period. He believed in the "push-pull" effect of painting: the aim is to take the eye in and out of the painting, excluding the effects of perspective and illusion. |
| *Acrylic paint* | a plastic paint that came into wide use in the early 1960s. It can be used on inexpensive cotton canvas without destroying the material (as oil paints do). It has the body of oil paints, the transparency of water-colour. |
| *Action Painting* | (see Abstract Expressionism). |
| *American realist tradition* | one of the central groups in the tradition of American painting. They believed in faithfully reproducing simple scenes of landscape, cityscape and daily life which tell the truth about people and their environment. The line follows from Thomas Eakins (1844-1916) to Edward Hopper (1882-    ). |
| *Art Nouveau* | developed in the 1890s, essentially in the field of furniture design, advertising and magazine illustration and architecture. The distinguishing quality was free-flowing ornamentation derived from plant forms. |
| *Automatic Painting* | (see Automatisme). |
| *Automatisme* | a term applied to the work done by Borduas and his followers during the late 1940s and the 1950s. It follows the principles of Abstract Expressionism, but it shows too the influence of surrealism. |
| *Barbizon School* | a mid-nineteenth-century group of landscape painters who painted near the village of Barbizon in France. They recorded nature in a natural way, but often with highly romantic overtones. They included Millet, Théodore Rousseau, and Diaz. |
| *Baroque* | a style developed in the seventeenth century, full of emotionalism, swooping curves and theatrical grandiloquence. |
| *Classical* | opposite of Romantic (which has usually taken the form of Expressionist painting in the twentieth century). In the classical style the object is to make rational statements that adhere to established principle. |
| *Collage* | a composition made by pasting different materials and objects (such as paper, string, cloth, photographs) to the surface of the work. |
| *Cubism* | between 1907 and 1914, Braque, Picasso, Juan Gris and Fernand Léger attempted to break down the surface of a painting to include the geometric volumes of a figure or object in a flat pattern. The first aspect was analytic Cubism, in which the subject was broken down to show many aspects of it at the same time. The second aspect was synthetic Cubism, which concentrated more on composition and surface texture than on the representation of an object. One result was the development of collage (or papier collé as these painters called it). |
| *Dutch School* | in the sixteenth and seventeenth centuries Dutch painters turned to the simple subject matter of their own environment, rendered in a direct, realistic technique. By the nineteenth century their Canadian imitators were painting dark, romanticised pictures that became known as The Brown Gravy School. |
| *Etching* | a method of print-making in which a metal plate is incised with acid to create a design, from which a printed impression can be taken. |
| *Expressionism* | a search for expressiveness of style by means of exaggerations and distortions of line and colour. |
| *Fauvisme* | a short-lived movement in France (1905-7). The word translates as the "Wild Beasts". The Fauves used violent colours to shock the senses. This meant bold simple forms and flat patterns. |
| *Genre painting* | painting in which the artist generally chooses as his subject, scenes of daily life. They are rendered in a realistic fashion, highly anecdotal. |

| | |
|---|---|
| *Impressionism* | the style of a group of painters in France in the 1870's, including Monet, Renoir, Pissaro and Degas, who discovered a new visual freedom and power by recording fleeting impressions of light, colour and movement in nature, using broken brushwork and highly-keyed colour. |
| *Laminated paper* | a method used to create a heavier surface for printing. Several pieces of paper are forced together, and in printing can stand greater pressure and produce a higher relief. |
| *Linocut* | a print-making process in which a piece of linoleum is cut away with knives or gouges, leaving the areas for inking standing in relief. |
| *Lithography* | a print-making process in which a heavy stone is marked with crayon and fixed with nitric acid. The surface is wetted and inked with an oil pigment. In the areas where the crayon and oily pigment come in contact, the ink adheres. Paper is applied under pressure and accepts the design of the inked areas. |
| *Magic Realism* | precise rendering of realistic detail, with strange super-real elements presented in such a way that they give a dream-like or timeless quality. The composition is usually extremely formal. |
| *National Style* | in Canada, a movement that developed between 1910 and 1930. It incorporated many of the trends of European art at that time (including *art nouveau),* and created an individual approach to Canadian landscape, particularly by the Group of Seven and members of the Canadian Group of Painters who came after them. |
| *Optical Art (or Op Art)* | a style popular in the late 1950s and 1960s that concentrates on optical effects to the exclusion of other content. Under a fixed gaze, the design gives the impression of calculated movement. The effect is based on the exact position of shapes and the interaction of colours. |
| *Pietà* | a representation of the Dead Christ supported on His Mother's lap, with or without mourning figures. |
| *Plasticiens* | a group of painters working in Montreal in the mid-1950s using geometrical ideas developed by Mondrian earlier in the century. Their emphasis was on pure colour and simple design without losing sensuality. |
| *Pop Art* | a term coined in the late 1950s to describe painters who take contemporary objects and try to give them new qualities. The most famous case is Andy Warhol's huge paintings of Campbell's soup labels. Some of the methods used by Pop artists include film and cartoon sequences, lettered slogans and comic strip balloons. Most Pop artists enjoy hugely everything about pop culture: mass media, advertising (which has picked up a great deal from Pop Art), the vulgarity of society, the noise and action as well as nostalgia for the 1930s and 1940s. |
| *Post-Painterly Abstraction* | a label given by New York art critic Clement Greenberg to artists in New York (and in Canada Jack Bush, Arthur McKay and Kenneth Lochhead) who paint abstract images, sometimes on unsized canvas, applying the paint as thinly as possible and using pure tones of colour. |
| *Still-Life* | an arrangement of inanimate objects. |
| *Surrealism* | a school of painting developed after World War I. These painters sought a way of expressing subconscious thoughts and dreams. They included Salvador Dali, Joan Miro and Paul Klee, who were fascinated by Freudian psychology. The name was coined by André Breton in 1924. |
| *Tachisme (Tachism)* | term used in France to describe Abstract Expressionism. In France the emphasis was on design and the touch of the paint to canvas. The style was much more elegant than its American counterpart. |
| *Touch Painting* | (see Tachisme). |
| *Trompe l'oeil* | a manner of representing the surface of an object so precisely that the eye is fooled; the effect simulates reality to the point of deception. |
| *Woodcut* | print-making method in which a wooden block is incised along the grain of the wood. The design stands in relief and generally has a hacked-out rough quality. |
| *Wood engraving* | requires a block of end-grain wood for a far more resistant surface, allowing the artist freedom to engrave more subtle lines than possible in a woodcut. |

# A calendar of painting in Canada

1860 Montreal Art Association (later Montreal Museum of Fine Arts) established.

1872 Ontario Society of Artists founded at the instigation of John Fraser, in Toronto.

1873 First exhibition of the OSA.

1876 Central Ontario Art School (later the Ontario College of Art) established in Toronto.

1880 Royal Canadian Academy established in Ottawa; Marquis of Lorne and Princess Louise, sponsors; Lucius O'Brien, first president.

First exhibition of the RCA. A group of these paintings were chosen to become the nucleus of the National Gallery collection.

National Gallery of Canada founded.

1882 *Picturesque Canada* published by G. M. Grant.

1883 Robert Harris commissioned to paint the Fathers of Confederation.

1886 CPR sends first transcontinental train across Canada with a group of painters aboard to record the trip.

1895 Maurice Cullen returns to Canada from France.

1905 Canadian Society of Graphic Art founded.

1910 Arts and Letters Club founded in Toronto (meeting place for members of the Group of Seven).

1911 Salon d'Automne in Paris includes paintings by Emily Carr.

1913 Armory Show, New York, includes work by David Milne.

Dr. J. M. MacCallum and Lawren Harris finance erection of The Studio Building in Toronto.

1917 Tom Thomson drowns.

Canadian War Artists commissioned.

1920 First show titled The Group of Seven. Members; Varley, Jackson, MacDonald, Lismer, Harris, Johnston, Carmichael.

1922 Ecole des Beaux Arts established in Quebec City.

1924 British Empire Exhibit at Wembley with five hundred entries from Canada.

Ecole des Beaux Arts established in Montreal.

Salon d'Automne, Paris, gives J. W. Morrice a retrospective exhibition, an honour accorded few North Americans.

1927 Exhibition of West Coast Indian Art organized by the National Gallery. Fifty canvases by Emily Carr included—her first official recognition in Canada.

1931 Edwin Holgate becomes a member of the Group of Seven.

1932 LeMoine FitzGerald becomes a member of the Group of Seven.

J. E. H. MacDonald dies.

1933 Group of Seven merged into the Canadian Group of Painters.

Jock Macdonald and Frederick Varley found the British Columbia College of Art.

1939 Contemporary Art Society founded by John Lyman in Montreal (members include Lyman, Borduas, Surrey and Roberts).

1940 Alfred Pellan returns to Canada.

1942 *Canadian Art* Magazine publishes its first issue.

Canadian War Artists commissioned.

1948 *Prisme d'Yeux* published in February by Pellan, de Tonnancour, Dumouchel, Bellefleur.

*Réfus Global* published by Borduas in August; among those who sign: Marcel Barbeau, Jean-Paul Mousseau, Jean-Paul Riopelle and Françoise Sullivan.

Borduas removed from his post at L'Ecole du Meuble.

1952 Painters Eleven formed in Toronto: Harold Town, Kazuo Nakamura, Alexandra Luke, Hortense Gordon, Walter Yarwood, Jack Bush, Jock Macdonald, Ray Mead, Oscar Cahén, Tom Hodgson and William Ronald. First exhibition of abstract art in Ontario.

Canada represented at the Venice Biennale for first time.

1953 Borduas leaves Canada.

1954 *Vie des Arts* publishes first issue.

1955 Guido Molinari opens a gallery in Montreal showing only non-objective art.

Greenwich (later renamed Isaacs) Gallery opens in Toronto.

Emma Lake Workshop founded in Saskatchewan.

1957 Canada Council formed.

1958 Canadian entry at the Guggenheim International is tied with the Japanese for best national entry.

1960 Borduas dies in Paris.

Jock Macdonald dies in Toronto.

Formation of La Relève, a group of young Montreal artists under thirty, separatist and anti-establishment in the art world.

Canadian entry judged best national entry at the Guggenheim International.

1962 Festival of Two Worlds, Spoleto, Italy, exhibition of Twenty-five Years of French-Canadian Painting.

1964 Musée d'Art Contemporain established in Montreal.

Toronto International Airport opened with $185,000 worth of Canadian paintings and sculpture.

HALF-TITLE ILLUSTRATIONS

Landscape      Arthur Lismer
               *Georgian Bay (Looking Across the Water)* / 1933   brush and ink on card   10¹/₂ x 13¹/₂
               Art Gallery of Toronto

Daily Life     Ernst Neumann
               *Artist and Critics* / n.d.   Wood Engraving   7-1/16 x 8-2/16
               National Gallery of Canada

The Cities     Kazuo Nakamura
               *Buildings* / 1954   ink drawing   14-3/8 x 20-3/8
               Art Gallery of Toronto

Faces and Figures   John Gould
                    *Reclining Nude* / 1961   dry brush drawing   18 x 23
                    Dr. G. A. Pengelly, Toronto

Feelings and Ideas   Richard Gorman
                     *All the Things you are, When you are What you are* / 1962   monoscreen   23¹/₂ x 17
                     Dr. and Mrs. S. L. Wax, Toronto

---

PRINTED IN ITALY

BOUND IN CANADA


*Text Type*       Melior and Optima

*Typographer*     Howarth & Smith Monotype Limited

*Printer*         Arnoldo Mondadori
                  Officine Grafiche, Verona, Italy

*Binding*         case printed by Sampson-Matthews Limited
                  made by the Ryerson Press
                  bound by T. H. Best Limited


*Photography*         Charles King

*Additional
Photography*          Lloyd Bloom, 58

                      Dennis Colwell, 28 (left), 49, 75, 108, 115

                      John Evans Photography, 55, 84 (lower)

                      Hollis Frampton, 30

                      Harvey Studios, 75 (upper), 90

                      John Reeves, 77, 93

                      Jack Shadbolt, 99

                      TDF Artists, 50, 92, 103

                      Robert Taylor, 64

                      Williams Brothers Photographers, 28 (right), 109 (left), 121